Be a Winner

—Moral Boosting Tips for a Confident and Successful Personality

O.P. Sharma

V&S PUBLISHERS

Published by:

V&S PUBLISHERS

F-2/16, Ansari Road, Daryaganj, New Delhi-110002
☎ 011-23240026, 011-23240027 • *Fax:* 011-23240028
Email: info@vspublishers.com • *Website:* www.vspublishers.com

Regional Office : Hyderabad
5-1-707/1, Brij Bhawan (Beside Central Bank of India Lane)
Bank Street, Koti, Hyderabad - 500 095
☎ 040-24737290
E-mail: vspublishershyd@gmail.com

Branch Office : Mumbai
Jaywant Industrial Estate, 2nd Floor-222, Tardeo Road
Opposite Sobo Central, Mumbai - 400 034
☎ 022-23510736
E-mail: vspublishersmum@gmail.com

Follow us on:

All books available at **www.vspublishers.com**

ISBN 978-93-813844-2-8
Edition 2016

Printed at : Param Offseters Okhla New Delhi-110020

Contents

Preface

The desire to bask in the glory of success is inherent in all human beings. Why do then some reach the peak of success and others are pushed into obscurity? A facile reply will be: They are darlings of destiny. Those who develop this brand of psyche are wedded to inaction which needless to say is the mother of failure. As a matter of fact we get what we deserve. In other words, fortune favours the prepared mind. This is by no means an ideal syrupy preaching. A peep into the lives of great personages bears testimony to the fact that fruits of labour are sweeter than gifts of fortune. This book intends to develop self-awareness in people and help them evolve their respective strategies and vision which may be enshrined thus: Intelligence and diligence are our best guarantors of success.

Most articles included in this volume were written by me years ago and appeared in magazines like Caravan (now Alive), Mirror, Art of Living, Careers Digest, Current Events, Social Welfare etc. I feel immensely indebted to them for publishing these articles.

I also owe a measure of gratitude to my borther-in-law Devki Nandan Sharma, who though much younger than me, had the wisdom to put me on the right track in my early life and his sister Janak Dulari my wife, who sustained my academic endeavours. V&S Publishers of this book too deserve to be highly appreciated for their earnest desire and effort to bring out this volume early.

O.P. Sharma

Are You Afraid of Your Mistakes?

Each day is a fresh day—look at it with hope and enthusiasm. Yesterday is over. Why not remove the garbage from your mind?

Only gods are infallible. Human beings, however intelligent, are liable to err. So we should learn to take mistakes in our stride and should not allow them to overwhelm us.

Mistakes are essential to progress. G.B. Shaw once said, "Man learns to skate by staggering, making a fool of himself. Indeed, he progresses in all things by resolutely making a fool of himself." From cave-life to modern civilised life is a story of trial and error. The people in the preceding ages, undaunted by the fear of mistakes, made inventions and discoveries that constitute the glory of modern civilisation.

Each time Nimmi, Kamla's 14-year old daughter, expresses her desire to prepare vegetables, her mother prevents her by saying, "You will spoil it." Kamla does not realise that her daughter cannot become expert in cooking without spoiling vegetables or burning a loaf. Parents should show tolerance when their children make mistakes. They should not resort to frequent snubbing to prevent the child from making mistakes.

Excessive scolding serves no useful purpose. It shatters the child's confidence and makes him peevish. It will not be surprising if he starts despising his parents. Let children do things and profit by the mistakes they make in the process. Not to allow your children to do things for fear of mistakes is to handicap their development.

Some persons do not take up a job on the plea that there are already superior persons in the profession. They conclude that the presence of the superior persons will spell their failure. They do not pause for a moment to think that the superior persons did not achieve perfection in their skill overnight. They, too, had to pass through a series of trials and errors before they could attain their present enviable positions. This should be enough to make beginners immune from the fear of being ridiculed by the superior persons. As a matter of fact, persons having superior skill do not ridicule the efforts of beginners. Only those who have remained imperfect due to their waywardness ridicule others.

If you have any plan to implement, do not be afraid of discussing it with your friends. If they point out any defects in your plan, you should not take it as jealousy on their part. Weigh their opinions objectively. It is quite possible that their advice may make your plan still better.

If you make a mistake, have the moral courage to acknowledge it and put it right. Mistakes do little harm if they are acknowledged and corrected without delay. Let mistakes remain unattended and they wil do untold harm to the task in hand and your reputation. Concealment of an error is no less undesirable. In case you camouflage your mistakes, you will have to resort to desperate lying to make your position invulnerable. When your lies are known to others which is only a matter of time, your dignity will be injured even more.

Nobody despises a person who has the moral courage to admit that he is wrong and is immediately prepared to rectify the error. What can you say to a person who candidly admits, "I beg your pardon. You are right, I misunderstood you. Please let me set the matter right."

It is bad to shift responsibility on to others for your own failures. Among students this tendency is often very marked. When they fail in an examination, they put the blame either on the teacher for his inefficient teaching or the fate. They never admit that they failed for lack of preparation. Some bosses make their subordinates scapegoats when their plans prove a flop. But when these succeed they pat only themselves and deny any credit to the subordinates. When we want to take credit for the success of a thing, we ought to bear responsibility for its miscarriage, too. To disown responsibility for failures is cowardice.

Brooding over past mistakes cripples positive thinking and creates unnecessary tension in the mind. You will do well to clear out the garbage of past mistakes from your mind. Begin next day's work with a fresh mind and vigour. You will surely find the way to success and happiness smooth.

■■

Put Your Emotions to Work

Emotions can increase your happiness and pleasure in life, or they can be blighters of joy and kill all incentive—the choice is all yours!

We all have emotions. They are inseparable from our life, just as fragrance is from a flower. They vitally affect our happiness. So we should learn to control them properly.

Emotions are of two types—good and bad. Good emotions make our personality attractive and increase happiness. We should cultivate them. Bad emotions prove blighters of happiness and killers of efficiency. We need to discard them.

Do you want to be loved and respected? You do. Then you should learn to like others. Respect the sentiments of the people around you and do not fail to appreciate their achievements when occasion demands. Genuine appreciation is a double blessing. It wins others' love and inspires the recipient to further achievements.

One day, my wife prepared some tasty dishes for dinner. I silently enjoyed the food. After a few moments, she asked me if I had not liked the dishes. I at once realised my folly and complimented her on her cooking. She beamed all over with joy.

Love is of great importance in all human relations. It is for the sake of love that parents suffer for their children, patriots make great sacrifices for their country, and people help follow-beings distressed by floods and earthquakes.

Other emotions which contribute to our happiness are courage, hope and patience. In all big enterprises of life, courage is essential. If a person does not acquire this quality, he will have to be content with modest achievements only. Fortune favours the brave.

There is none who can claim immunity from failures. Failures bring a lot of misery in their wake. In such circumstances, it is the oar of hope that takes one's boat out of troubled waters. You can draw ambitious plans, but without patience you cannot carry them out. You can well imagine the consequences of the fiasco of a big business venture in which you showed lack of patience halfway.

Fear, anger and hate should not be allowed free play. Otherwise these can wreck our happiness.

Fear undermines courage and paralyses action. It flings open the gates of misery. I know of a young man who did not take his examination several times for fear of failure. On every occasion, he found one excuse or the other to justify his action. He complained that his mind did not work properly. In fact, nothing was wrong with his mind. He had developed the habit of distrusting his mental faculty.

He can pull himself out of this unfortunate situation only through adequate preparation and then going through the examination with confidence. By avoiding the examination, he cannot hope to change failure into success.

There is the case of a young woman who had miscarried several times. Some of her acquaintances continue to din into her ears that maternity is a risky thing. They often quote instances of women who have lost their lives in child birth. She now finds herself quite diffident to face the situation. For many years she had been deprived of the pleasure of having a child. She should tell herself that she will survive maternity just as women who advise her have survived. The best course to conquer fear is to face the object of fear with courage.

Anger is another negative emotion. It paralyses thinking. A man who has not tamed anger creates a social desert around him. There is an elderly woman in our neighbourhood who flares up at the slightest provocation. She scolds her children and servants for mere trifles. She has converted her house into a virtual hell. Her servants and children are happy if she is away even for a day. Last year, her son and daughter-in-law came to spend their holiday with her. But even they were unable to put up with her temper and left after a few days.

Vijay opened a general merchant's shop at a most advantageous point in our city. Everyone thought that he would be a success soon. For a few months, it ran smoothly and seemed to fulfil their expectations. But suddenly his business ran into rough weather. Vijay started quarrelling with his customers and sometimes abused them if after seeing his goods they did not purchase them. Naturally, people did not like his treatment and withdrew their patronage. Ultimately he had to close the shop.

If you want to lead a socially happy life you should not hate your fellow-beings. If people around you feel that you hate them, your company will repel them like acrid smoke. If you are a business executive you cannot hope to get cooperation of your subordinates by hating them. If you resort to punitive measures against them there is every possibility of their going on a strike. This can put even your job in jeopardy.

Love succeeds where money and punishment fail. Of course hate is an intractable emotion. It is not easy to root it out. But you can surely get along with others smoothly by keeping it under leash.

But this does not mean that you should totally inhibit your emotions. In fact, total suppresion of emotions is as bad as indulging in emotional sprees.

By suppressing emotions completely, you will make many good aspects of your life charmless. For example, you cannot subtract feelings from marriage, friendship and work. It is the emotion of love that keeps the spouses together after their sexual desire is satisfied. So is the case with friendship. You meet a good many people in your life, but only a few become your friends and others remain mere acquaintances. It is because you share your feelings only with those who are your friends. If you involve yourself emotionally in some work, it becomes a pleasure rather than drudgery.

On the other hand, overplaying of emotions is also undesirable. For instance, some people in their moments of failure try to attract others' attention by arousing self-pity. By doing so, they often make themselves the object of ridicule rather than sympathy. If you have suffered failure in one sphere, you can comfort yourself by thinking of your success elsewhere. But you shoud avoid enlisting the sympathy of others unnecessarily.

One prefers the company of good persons because it brings happiness. So is the case with good emotions. Why not live with them! It is easy to cultivate good emotions. Dwell on the desired emotion in thought, see it as desirable and you will possess it. When you have acquired the wished-for emotion, half the battle is won.

Prosperous and happy people have consciously cultivated good emotions and tamed bad ones. They have not received the gift of good emotions from God. Ask them; they will confirm it.

How to Like Your Work

Not the criticism of your job, environment or colleagues, etc., but keen interest in work will help you to go up...

Men and women have to work for a living. Most of them work only for material gain, while others work not only for material gain but also for the pleasure they derive from the work they do.

Two factors determine one's attitude to work: the amount of work and one's ablity. Excess of work is certainly irksome. However energetic a man may be, he cannot work like an automaton. If a person has adequate skill for a job, he will do it efficiently and joyfully. If he is not so equipped, he will do the job inefficiently. Such a person will be a liability to his employer rather than an asset. It will not be surprising if the employer gets rid of him soon.

While choosing a vocation, you should keep in view your ability. Young people are often tempted by certain jobs because they are lucrative. They completely ignore the requirements of the job and take a headlong plunge. The consequences can be disastrous. It is essential to remember that ambition without talent cannot lead to success.

Rajesh set-up a large motor parts store. He hoped to become a big businessman, but as he had no aptitude for the line, he discovered after a year that nearly half of his investment had disappeared by way of loss.

You should choose a profession after considering its various aspects. Once you have chosen it, stick to it. There are people who get disenchanted with any job they take up and develop an itch to change. Such a disposition is detrimental to success. To climb higher in any profession, you need vast experience and efficiency. You cannot acquire these qualities by changing your profession too frequently. You may, at best, gain preliminary knowledge about other jobs but that will not help you to go up. In this age when specialisation is the universal cry, a jack of all trades and master of none cannot hope to occupy an enviable position.

Love your work. Never condemn it. Love of work fosters the spirit of perseverance. Its rewards are amazing. It is through work that you can realise your ambition. Again, it is work that enables you to show your talent. The achievements of great scientists, artists and social reformers illustrate this point.

Madame Curie was born in Poland at a time when women were not allowed to study science. When she sought admission to Cracow University, she was told that science was not a thing in which women should meddle. She was offered a seat in cookery classes! She went to Sorbonne University in France to study science. Here, after several years of arduous research, she discovered radium and won the Nobel Prize for her unique achievement. She was able to make this outstanding discovery because she was in love with her work and refused to be deterred by difficulties.

Perhaps, the world would have remained afflicted with the curse of malaria if Ronald Ross had not persisted in his research in the face of formidable difficulties. For many years, success eluded him and when at last he found the cause of malaria, he was so weary of the ceaseless toil that he did not appreciate the discovery until he had slept. Nursing would not have become a noble profession for women but for the dedication of Florence Nightingale.

Undesirable Disposition

There are people who go into raptures over the virtues of other jobs but condemn their own. Such a disposition is undesirable. Rakesh is a lecturer in physics. He has brilliant educational qualifications and an impressive personality. All these qualities should have made him a good teacher. But the ten years that he has put in the profession have benefited him little. The reason is that he is absolutely indifferent to his job. He rues the day when he joined the teaching profession. He feeds himself on the illusion that one day he will become a fat salaried manager of some large firm.

Ramesh is a colleague of Rakesh. He joined the profession only three years back, but has already come to be known as an efficient teacher. Not only students but his colleagues recognise his devotion to work.

There are some jobs which do not provide opportunities for advancement of talented persons. If you are placed in such a job, you have a genuine cause for dissatisfaction. But because you are not getting a stimulating and challenging opportunity that your talent demands, you should not try to remedy it by detesting your work. That is no cure. It can only make you unhappy. The way out of such a situation is to keep watching patiently for an opportunity and avail yourself of it when it comes.

Environment also makes work pleasant or unpleasant. Favourable environment inspires a worker to achieve higher efficiency and output. Unfavourable environment dampens all zeal for work. If you are convinced that your environment is extremely inhospitable, you will do well to seek a change. But you should not become over-sensitive to environment. If you do so, you will not feel happy anywhere. That your environment should be free from all irritations. Abraham Lincoln, Gandhi and Nehru would not have succeeded in their goals, had they waited for ideal environment.

You can make your environment tolerable by adapting yourself to it. You should avoid conflict with your colleagues. You should not belittle them. Disparagement of others will trap you in the vicious circle of condemnation and counter-condemnation. Co-operation of your colleagues will go a long way in making your surroundings congenial.

Another important point is that you should not criticise

your boss before your colleagues, particularly before those who are intimate with the boss. They are likely to carry tales to gain his favour at your cost. That will embitter your relations with the boss. If you are antagonistic towards your boss, you cannot hope to get any joy out of the job, despite all your ability and efficiency.

Some people feel disenchanted with their jobs because they are not fat-salaried. Mohan is earning Rs 6000 a month. But he is dissatisfied. He thinks that persons of his ability and qualifications are gettig much higher salaries in other professions. He does not consider for a moment the leisure his present job provides him. He utilises his leisure to go on picnics with his family. He also finds time to play games. But he considers all these benefits trivial.

He fails to see that the high-salaried man who is his idol gets little leisure. He rarely joins his family at meals. He cannot go on picnics with his family. A higher salary usually means more tension and worries. Perhaps, no sensible man would like to forgo his peace of mind just to get a few chips more.

If you are always after work you will soon be overcome by monotony. To save yourself from monotony, you should have leisure to pursue hobbies. The time which you spend in pursuing hobby is not wasted. A hobby relieves you of the tensions and feeling of tiredness that your work fosters. Thereafter, you can resume your work with renewed vigour and freshness.

Do Not Be Afraid of Criticism

The man who achieves things, is not the one who goes to pieces on his first encounter with others' disapproval.

Shyam won the first prize in a debate. He was bubbling with joy. His joy further multiplied when his friends congratulated him on his brilliant performance. He rushed home to share the happy news with the members of his family.

But Shyam's mood of buoyancy was suddenly killed next day. A college friend, Manohar, told him that some boys were remarking that he did not deserve the prize and that it was an instance of favouritism. On hearing this, all cheerfulness vanished, and a wave of anger gripped him. He looked like a shrivelled plant in summer. The reason why Shyam felt so unhappy by the criticism of his companions is not far to seek. Most of us expect one and all performance almost to the extent of adultation. When this does not happen, it hurts us.

Shyam, however, does not realise that no one escapes critcism altogether. History provides numerous examples of great men whose achievements were laughed to scorn in the beginning. George Washington, the liberator of America, was denounced as a hypocrite and impostor. A newspaper cartoon depicted him on a guillotine, the big knife ready to cut off his head. Crowds jeered at him and hissed as he rode through the streets. Edward Jenner is another great man who was ridiculed. Yet he is the man to whom people of the world are now grateful for the boon of the smallpox vaccination. But when Jenner was engaged in the discovery of the vaccination, even doctors, not to speak of ordinary people, scoffed at him.

Criticism hurts your self-respect and naturally you feel tempted to retaliate. If you are a very sensitive and honest person, the reaction is all the more sharp. Retaliatino is not always practicable. It is not necessary that your critics are living at the same place where you are living. Even if your critics are within easy reach, it is not advisable to reply to them. If you choose to reply, most of your time will be consumed by planning retaliation and counter-retaliation. Thus you will have little time for any worthwhile pursuit. Above all this negative thinking poisons the mind thoroughly. Retaliation may give you a momentary thrill, but ultimately, you feel immensely miserable.

Whenever you are criticised you will do well to follow the strategy which Lincoln adopted towards his critics. During the American Civil War, Lincoln was severely criticised. But he did not lose his nerve and start hurling counter jibes at his critics. Instead, he displayed tremendous tranquillity of mind. The only reply he gave to his critics was this: "If I were to try to read, much less to answer, all the attacks made on me, this shop might as well be closed for any other business. I do the very best I know...the very best I can, and I mean to keep on doing so until the end. If the end brings me out all right, then what is said against me won't matter. If the end brings me out wrong, then ten angels swearing

I was right would make no difference."

Lincoln, as we know, is hailed as a saviour of America. His critics had to reconcile themselves to his great achievement. They got convinced that their clamour could not obscure the worth of his greatness.

You should not let your critics have the upper hand and block your way to progress. Sheila kept her critics at bay by turning a deaf ear to them. When she was preparing herself for the IAS examination, many persons of her locality started poking fun at her. Did she feel embarrassed? Not the least. In fact, she showed as if the critics did not seem to exist for her. Finally, she was selected as an IAS officer. Her distinctive achievement served as a rebuff to her critics. Some of them became her articulate admirers even.

> **The Chimney-sweep**
>
> Som critics are like chimney-sweepers; they put out the fire below, and frighten the swallows from their nests above; they scrape a long time in the chimney, cover themselves with soot, and bring nothing away but a bag of cinders, and then sing out from the top of the house, as if they had built it.
>
> —*Longfellow*
>
> Of all mortals a critic is the silliest; for, inuring himself to examine all things, whether they are of consequence or not, he never looks upon anything but with a design of passing sentence upon it; by which means he is never a companion, but always a censor.
>
> —*Steele*

Criticism is often a disguised compliment to one's ability. Talented persons always do something out of the ordinary. Their activities sometimes rudely jolt the ignorance of other people or are an assault on the social evils. The conformists look upon their activities as a sacrilege. They show their resentment by releasing a barrage of criticism against them. Ishwar Chander Vidyasagar is now hailed as a great social reformer. But when he assailed the Hindu custom which prohibited widows to remarry, he was severely denounced. Gandhiji had to encounter tremendous hostility in his campaign against untouchability. Both these leaders displayed great courage in the face of monstrous opposition.

Galileo attacked Aristotle's scientific observations by asserting that two different weights released simultaneously from the same height would fall to the ground at the same time. "Nobody but a fool can believe that a feather and a cannon ball will travel downward through the space at the same speed," remarked the adversaries of Galileo.

But Galileo did not feel disheartened. On the contrary, in the midst of the jeering crowds he went up the leaning tower of Pisa and demonstrated the truth of his observations by dropping two balls—one ten pounds in weight and another one pound in weight. When his detractors saw both the balls hit the ground simultaneously, they were dumbfounded.

What sort of people criticise others? Those who criticise others usually are petty-minded persons. They do not have any significant achievements to their credit. When they find others achieving one success after another, they begin to burn with jealousy. Unable to compete with them, they try to obstruct their progress through carping criticism. By pointing out others' failings, they try to cover up their own inadequacies and clutch at false importance. Schopenhauer rightly says, "Vulgar people take huge delight in the faults and follies of great men."

As They See Us

Criticism stings us much because we have not cultivated the habit of looking at it in the proper spirit. We have built up a wrong image of ourselves. We think we are infallible. We want others to accept us as paragons of perfection. But others judge us by their own standards. Obviously, they discover some faults in us. But most of us are reluctant to see even the glaring chinks in our armour. If anyone happens to bring our faults to our notice, we dismiss him by saying, "His remarks are born of prejudice."

The result is that we continue to cling to our foibles which hold back our progress. If you do not dismiss others' remarks about yourself in a fit of anger and seize the opportunity for sincere appraisal of yourself, you are sure to find some foibles which you would like to get rid soon as you start making earnest efforts to increase the number of your handicaps, your popularity will touch a new high and your activities will receive ready approval from others.

Recently I visited a leading shop in our city which has a beautiful motto displayed on its front wall. The motto reads: "If you are dissatisfied with our service, tell us. If satisfied, tell others." Actually, all the big commercial establishments try to redress the grievances of their customers. They maintain their public relations departments to study the reactions of their customers. Their sensitiveness of public opinion brings them rich dividends.

Truly speaking the march of our civilization is itself sustained by healthy criticism. From time to time, we create new things and values of life and reject the old ones. All this clearly points out how indispensable unbiased criticism is for our progress. In the absence of criticism, complacency sets in and the march of civilization reaches its dead end.

Next time when you are criticised, do not fly into a rage. Instead, think seriously if you can do something to remove the cause of your critic's annoyance with you. It is not that easy to cultivate the habit of self-restraint. But the man worth his salt is not afraid of the effort when the reward is worthwhile. Of course, it is not necessary that your critic's view is the correct one. It is just possible that your adversary is trying to tarnish your image out of sheer jealousy. In that case, you should kill his slander by observing dignified silence.

Criticism will also cease to sting you if you adopt a realistic approach towards life. Remember that even if your work is inspired by the best motives, there will always be some persons to throw mud at you. So you should learn to take a bit of criticism in your stride. Norman Vincent Peale suggests perhaps the most pragmatic way to cope with criticism, "Just as some people rub us the wrong way for no particular reason, so we rub some others the wrong way. If you face this simple truth, you will not be unduly disturbed by a certain amount of unpopularity."

■■

Turn Failure into Success

Only a ceaseless struggle against failure gives life any meaning, charm or joy; for it is only dead man who meets no failure–nor success too!

Life is a mixed bag of joys and sorrows. Anyone who says that life is all agony is a cynic. But the man who considers life a bed of roses deludes himself no less. Such a person usually succumbs to the first blow of adversity and allows failure to overwhelm him. But the man who has learnt to endure the blows of misfortune rises to amazing heights of fame and glory.

Raju expected fate to accord him a red carpet welcome all the time. For some time, fate did shower favours on him lavishly. Later, Raju set up a small business. At that time, everyone predicted that he would be eliminated by competition very soon. But he did not pay any heed to his critics. He put his heart and soul into his work. Within a few years, his business became a roaring success. Now all those who had proclaimed his doom were dazzled by his excellent performance and became vociferous in their praise of him.

Wrapped in the halo of power and prestige which prosperity brought in its wake, Raju felt he was on the top of the world. It did not occur to him that a dark cloud could appear on the horizon of his life.

When Raju was blissfully wallowing in prosperity, all of a sudden slump gripped industry. His business, too, was hit. The huge profits which were flowing into his pockets began to vanish. After some time, he began to suffer losses. But this he could not stomach.

It did not console him that he was not the only victim of the slump but there were many others in the same predicament. He did not pause to think that the present situation could be a temporary phase in his life, and his intelligence which in the past had put him on the pinnacle of prosperity could enable him to tide over the crisis he was facing. All his friends assured him of better times ahead. But nothing helped him to get rid of his obsession about a dark future. Unable to bear the strains of frustration, he committed suicide.

As a contrast, Prakash reacted differently when he fell on bad days. He did not let failure have the last laugh. He had served with distinction as a lecturer in a non-Government college for eight years. Obviously, he thought his job was quite secure. But suddendly, the number of the students in his faculty dwindled. Finding the faculty unprofitable, the managing committee decided to abolish it, and he became jobless.

Unemployment did not hold out any terror for him. He had some landed property to fall upon. What pinched him most was the humiliation caused by his unjust dismissal. The caustic comments of some of his colleagues also added to his misery. Some said he was not competent to get a job elsewhere.

The unkind comments of others hurt Prakash's sensitive mind. For a few days, he felt immensely miserable. Even dark thoughts about committing suicide began to torment his mind. But when he thought of the plight of his loving wife after his death, he desisted from the abominable act of killing himself.

With the passing of time, his dismissal began to lose its sting. His confidence in his ability revived. He started searching for a new job. After a few unsuccessful efforts in the beginning, he finally succeeded in getting a job. His new job was not as gainful as the previous one. But the love and respect of his new colleagues compensated the monetary loss. He became totally oblivious of the monetary loss. He did not allow the crisis to break him.

Kailash's case is different. He wants to earn fabulous amounts of money. He is fully convinced that this is possible only through business. But he is hesitant to set up a business, as his friend has suffered heavy losses in business. Haunted by the phobia of imaginary failure, he has been drifting for the last five years. He is forgetting the essential fact that there is no magic ladder to success.

A farmer who reaps a bumper crop has to first brace up to face the hazards of the pests and drought. As a matter of fact, no one can hope to achieve significant success in any walk of life without taking risks. "A man cannot grasp a star if he does not reach for it," says a writer. "Neither will he get food for his table, nor shelter for his family nor knowledge and skill in the exercise of his talents by merely visualizing them. The only man that life rains down on him is that which he has merited and produce through his physical and mental efforts."

This is no copy-book maxim. However expert in the art of eating, everyone spills something or other. A wise man never cries over a slip. He knows that efficiency on which success depends is the outcome of commission of mistakes and their correction. J.S. Mursel says: The number of times you try is not the important consideration. The important consideration is the intelligence with which you try and, above all, what you yourself discover from your tries."

On the face of it, failure appears unpleasant to us. But, in reality, it is a blessing in disguise. Failures develop in us the valuable traits of character like fellow-feeling and courage. One who has suffered himself never mocks at others' setbacks. He is fully aware that the road to success is rugged and the man who pursues that road will inevitably get jerks and jolts. Instead of scoffing at others' failures, he shows sympathy and tenders unbiased advice. Napoleon Hill says, "Failure is Nature's great crucible in which she burns the dross from the human heart and so purifies the metal of the man that it can stand the test of hard usage."

Like fellow-feeling, courage, too, is developed when man is confronted with difficult situations in life. We all know that a kite rises against the wind and not with it. It is needless to stress the importance of courage in life because the things of lasting value in this world have all been done by the people with vision and courage.

There is the classic example of Napoleon who said, "There shall be no Alps" and led his army across the mountains down into Italy and to victory. Another illustrious example is of George Stephenson's courage. It was sheer mortal courage which enabled him to test the efficacy of the safety lamp he had invented for the use of the miners. Determined to give it a thorough trial, he surprised his friends by descending into a mine and enquiring for the most dangerous passage.

He was told of one level that was filled with gas and at once started forward to make his test. The rest of the party shrank back and got into safe quarters. Obviously, George Stephenson moved in the jaws of death. But his heart did not quail, nor his hand tremble. Having arrived at the place of danger, he stretched out his lamp in the full rush of the explosive gas and patiently awaited the result. At first, the flame of the lamp increased, then it wavered, waned and gradually expired. There was no explosion.

Stephenson thus discovered a tolerably soft means of lighting up a mine without risk of igniting its combustible air. In other words, he had provided for the safety of hundreds and hundreds of lives. This was the first practical miners' safety lamp.

Besides making great achievements possible, courage

enhances a man's prestige in the eyes of the opposite sex, too. In last war, one woman said to another: "I would rather be a soldier's widow than a coward's wife."

Courage also wards off despair, the enemy of success. But to make success doubly sure, you must make correct assessment of your mental and physical powers. For instance, if you nurse an ambition to reach the summit in your chosen field of work withlout taking your capacities into account, obviously you are courting failure. Moreover, to be successful, you do not have to be the best. Remember, no two persons can be the Prime Ministers of a country simultaneoulsy. No two persons can be captains of a team simultaneously. Someone has to accept the second place. If by any quirk of fate, you are denied the first place, despite your sincere efforts and calibre, you should not let frustration wreck your peace of mind.

Richard Nixon suffered two successive defeats at the polls as a Presidential candidate. The experts forecast that he had been condemned to political wilderness for ever. But he did not allow frustration to overwhelm him. Instead, he continued to woo the voters with unabated zeal and, ultimately, succeeded in making one of the most amazing political comebacks in the history.

If you want to scare away failure and bask in the glory of success, learn to preserve your peace of mind in the face of heavy odds. A writer beautifully sums up the matter "All the water in the ocean can sink a ship unless the water starts getting inside. All the troubles in the world cannot sink a human being unless those troubles invade his inner life."

■■

The Miraculous Power of Imagination

The wonderful creative faculty when, properly used, enables man to convert even a roaring water-fall into a source of light and power.

The dictionary defines the word 'imagination' as follows: 'The act of constructive intellect in grouping the materials of knowledge or thought into new, original and rational systems; the constructive creative faculty embracing poetic, artistic, philosophic and scientific thinking.' Imagination is of two types—synthetic and creative. Synthetic imagination is interpretative. It can examine facts, concepts and ideas, and it can create new combinations and plans out of these. We all possess synthetic imagination in varying degrees. But creative imagination is possessed by the artists, writers, musicians and scientists of the highest order only.

Both synthetic imagination and creative imagination become more alert with use just as any organ or muscle of the body develops through use. This fact has been confirmed by the various researches of the psychologists. Hence the man who values success in life and does not want to live in disgraceful obscurity, never neglects his imaginative faculty. He is fully aware that imagination is the workshop of the human mind and, all ideas concerning great fortunes are the products of this workshop. If the workshop is ill-equipped, the products will be naturally sub-standard. Consequently, the dividends of the sub-standard products will be poor. But an ambitious person is never content with the crumbs of success. He wants to enjoy a sumptuous feast instead.

History is replete with examples of men who by developing their imaginative faculty have made memorable contribution to the progress of mankind. Niagara Falls was nothing but a great mass of roaring water until a man of imagination harnessed it and converted the wasted energy into electric current that now turns the wheels of industry. Before this man of imagination came along, millions of people had seen and heard those roaring falls but lacked the imagination to harness them.

Again, it was because Morse saw in his imagination a better way of communication than by post that he was able to give the telegraph to the world. We have telephone because Bell could imagine something better even than the telegraph. This is not all. We owe our whole modern civilization to the cumulative results of the efforts made by the great men of vision. If these great men had not developed their imaginative faculty fully and used it profitably, we should be still living as savage in the caves.

The use of imaginative faculty is not confined to scientific discoveries only. It equally pervades artistic, economic and political fields. Kalidas and Rabindranath Tagore have shot India into literary fame through their immortal works. Leonardo da Vinci's painting "Mona Lisa" bears an eloquent testimony to the unique fertility of his imagination. Men of imagination become leaders in the field of business and industry. Besides earning profits for themselves, they provide jobs to millions of people and thus add to the prosperity of their country. In the political field, too, there is hardly any place for a man who lacks imagination. Gandhi ji, J.S. Mill and a host of other people who are today remembered for their political wisdom had learnt to put their imagination to work in an excellent manner in their chosen fields.

Imagination helps us no less in managing the ordinary affairs of life efficiently as in making the great scientific discoveries. The touch of imagination transforms a dull and drab life into a charming one. For several years, our town was without any park and proper drainage system. This was not for lack of money. The fact was that the men who were at the helm of affairs these years lacked the necessary imagination to develop the skill properly.

Some years back, a young man full of enthusiasm and imagination became the Administrator of the Muñicipal Commitee. And now our town has been transformed into a beautiful place. We have a beautiful park now where men, women and children flock together and enjoy a delightful evening. No longer do we have stinking garbage heaps at every street corner. The roads and streets look spick and span. Indeed, it is a sheer delight to walk on them.

A housewife with imagination can perform a similar miracle on the home front. Everyone who visits Sheela, admires her housekeeping. All this is due to her imaginative approach to work. Besides cooking for her large family, she looks after three kids. She also washes clothes herself. Despite all these strenuous chores, she manages to find time to keep her house tidy. Unlike Bina, she does not allow things to lie at sixes and sevens.

Paula has a small family of three. She also has a maid-servant to assist her in her domestic chores. Yet her house looks like a lumber room. In her house, you will find unclean clothes hanging here and there. Costly decoration pieces which should have been the pride of her drawing room, lie huddled together on a shelf accumulating dust. In short, her drawing-room looks repulsive. All this happens because she does not use her imagination in managing her affairs. To keep up with the Joneses she wastes her time in gossiping and visiting friends and movies. She does not realize that house-keeping has greater importance.

Is imagination a divine gift? Certainly not. Everyone of us is gifted with imagination. It may be true that we all are not able to develop our imagination to the extent of making rare artistic things or scientific discoveries. But we all can certainly develop our imagination faculty to the extent that it brings us a fairly reasonable measure of success. If in the beginning your efforts do not bear fruit in cultivating imagination, you need not feel discouraged. Even the great playwright, Kalidas did not have the gift of keen imagination offered to him on a silver platter. As you know, in his early life he was noted for his idiocy; he was once actually found cutting the very branch on which he was sitting. But later on, through his patient and presistent efforts at cultivating his imagination, he swung the pendulum from idiocy to celebrity. You can follow his suit with advantage.

Poise is Power

This power dwells right in you. You have just to develop it.

Ranjit embarked upon a business venture with high hopes. To ensure success he invested a sizable amount and set-up the shop in that part of the city which was a focal point for customers. Besides, he made a partner who had long experience in that line of business. Success came to him instantly in ample measure. He had a bumper sale and earned huge profits. Quick success convinced Ranjit that the day was not far away when he would be willing in wealth.

But unexpectedly there set in a general slump. The business community began to experience financial difficulties. Ranjit too did not remain unaffected. But he had not anticipated such an unpleasant turn in his affairs. So, he was wholly unprepared to face the situation. He lost serenity. He began to lose temper with his partner over trifles. If any customer did not make a purchase, he showered a volley of abuses on him before he stepped out of the shop.

Lost Hopes

His partner advised Ranjit not to lose temper with customers as this could have adverse effect on their business. He also pointed out to Ranjit that the slump would not continue for ever and above all others were affected. But Ranjit brushed aside this advice as childish. Very soon all stopped patronising his shop. This created serious differences between Ranjit and his partner. Eventually the business had to be wound up. All hopes of Ranjit for piling up money evaporated into the thin air.

Lack of equanimity affects family happiness no less than professional success. Pushpa's husband is a highly paid executive. She has two charming children—a boy and a girl. Besides, she has a big bungalow with modern amenities and a number of servants to dance around to her tune. Obviously she should be a very happy person. But her irritability has made her home a veritable hell. She flies into rage over trifles...At the slightest provocation she begins to chide her servants, children and even her husband. Her husband and children prefer to spend most of their time outside their home! Her unpopularity with her neighbours? They call her a witch.

Sheela is just the opposite of Pushpa. She is serving as a public relations officer. Naturally, she has a very busy schedule of work in her office. But she does not let her rough and tumble in her office schedule disturb her mental equilibrium. She has learnt to take problems and difficulties in her stride. Proof? She never utters a harsh word to anyone even when she is hard-pressed by work. In fact from her sweet and courteous behaviour it appears that she has no problem to face. At home also she does not go to pieces if things go wrong. She discusses every problem with a calm mind and succeeds in solving it. If children and servants make mistakes, she does not pour out her wrath over them. She knows that this does not mend matters. So instead of rebuking she gently advises them to be more careful in future. Everyone in the house takes care to heed her advice. Her serenity has brought her a rich reward. She is tremendously popular both at home and in the office.

Vishnu too owes his success and popularity to his mental equanimity. As a sales manager he is often confronted with ticklish problems. But he does not let them shatter his mental balance. For example, if the sale of a producer is sagging, he does not blame his supervisors and chide them for this. On the contrary, he discusses the problem with them in a cordial manner. This usually helps him in solving the problem. In this way Vishnu succeeds not only in tiding over a difficult situation but also earns respect and cooperation from his colleagues.

Keep Cool

Evidently to achieve success and happiness one needs poise in all walks of life. But the higher you climb the ladder of success the higher degree of poise you need. If you hold a top position, there is every possibility that you will be under heavy fire. Your opponents will employ all weapons to lash you with. They will exaggerate your minor faults. They will try to malign you even by attributing imaginary lapses to you. They will play up your alleged lack of devotion to duty. They may even go to the extent of branding you immoral. In such cricumstances if you keep your cool to take wind out of the sails of your adversaries, they can not deprive you of your success.

Bear in mind, however able a person may be, he cannot marshal his forces and do his best in an argument when he loses control of himself. In fact he is at the mercy of his opponents who can make him look ridiculous.

The late US President Cleveland did not let his opponents have a last laugh. During presidential campaign he was severely denounced, even ostracized by a certain section of the society. When he was elected everybody seemed to expect that he would be extremely disconcerted and unnerved during inaugural ceremonies at Washington as he had been under terrific fire for long. But he displayed amazing serenity.

J.J. Ingalls describes it thus: "There sat this man before me, wholly undisturbed by the multitudes, calmly waiting to perform his part in the great drama, just as an actor awaits his cue to appear on the stage.

"I looked for him to produce a manuscript but he did not; and as he progressed in clear and distinctive tones without hesitation, I was amazed. With sixty millions of people, yes with the entire civilized world looking on, this man had the courage to deliver an inaugural address, making him President of the United States as coolly and unconcernedly as if he were addressing a Board meeting."

Shock Absorber

Saint just rightly says, "Keep cool and you command everybody" Seneca too says the same thing: "Most powerful is he who has himself in his power." Truly speaking poise is to man what a shock-absorber is to an automobile. If an automobile is fitted with good shock-absorbers, the traveller does not suffer any inconvenience even on a rugged road. Similarly a man of poise goes through life cheerfully undaunted by difficulties.

While a controlled mind brings fame and glory to a person, an uncontrolled mind pushes him into the chasm of shame and suffering. Crimes are perpetrated by the people who have not learnt to control their mind. Even the slightest provocation is enough to make them go berserk.

You may be thinking that the power of poise which plays such a vital role in life must be something illusory. But it is not. In fact this power dwells right in you. You have just to develop it. Remember, even gold—the most precious metal, is useless as long as it lies buried in the bowels of earth. But the moment you possess it by digging, it covers with the halo of affluence—one of the most cherished things in life.

Now pause to think: Are you sincerely in love with your ambitions? Do you aspire to attain peak in your chosen profession? If so, you just can't neglect cultivating the power of poise. ■■

Get Rid of the Tyranny of Bad Habits

Bad habits are tyrants. They take all the joy out of life and make it an unbearable burden. Shed them off; you will claim a clean, springing laughter again.

Some years ago, Prem Chand set-up a modest business. At the time of starting his business, he resolved to lead a life of austerity so that ploughing back his profits, he might make his venture a flourishing one within a short time. His family members cooperated with him by following his example. The scheme worked wonderfully well. Financial

success came to Prem Chand in such a large measure that everyone in the town was startled.

In the wake of the financial success, everyone in the family expected that they would enjoy its fruits in the form of a raised standard of living. But Prem Chand did not bother about the standard of living of his family. In fact, the more profits he earned, the more close-fisted he became. He turned down even the most reasonable demands of his family members by saying, "You don't know how money is earned."

Sometimes, his stinginess bordered on inhumanity. Once his youngest son fell ill. His wife pleaded with him that the boy should be taken to some good doctor as his condition was serious. He simply told her that modern doctors knew nothing except extorting money. He further advised her that she should give some home made medicines and the boy would recover very soon. This did not satisfy his wife. She protested against his indifference. But he did not pay any heed to it. After a few days the boy expired. The tragedy filled his wife with bitterness against him. Now she frequently hurls accusations at him for causing the untimely death of the boy. To console her, he says that that was the will of God and she should calmly accept the inevitable. This irritates his wife all the more because despite the tragedy, he has not realized the futility of his stinginess. He continues to neglect the welfare of his family as before. Consequently, there are frequent conflicts and seething discontent in the family.

Kedar, too, once started his business on a very modest scale. Today he owns one of the biggest commercial houses in the town. But like Prem Chand, he does not believe in accumulating money at the cost of the family happiness. He forbids extravagance, but allows his family to enjoy reasonable comforts. His outlook on life is that money is for man and not the reverse. This is the reason that he contributes generously to many public welfare programmes of his town. His reward is great. Everyone holds him in high esteem in the town.

Evidently if good habits have a grip on one's life, it is a

matter of joy. But if bad habits have a similar grip, it is a matter of deep concern. Bad habits are tyrants. They take all the joy out of life and make it an unbearable burden. Habits do not grow all of a sudden. They are the outcome of the repetition of our acts over the years. A popular saying goes like this: If we sow an act, we reap a character. Thus we should avoid hasty and ill-considered acts as they have far-reaching effects.

But some persons do not seem to realize the implications of their acts. A few years back, when Manohar had his first taste of wine, his friends strongly advised him to keep himself away from drinking. Manohar promised not to repeat the act. On a subsequent occasion when his friend found him drinking again, he reminded Manohar of his promise. Manohar replied, "I drink only occasionally for recreation in the company of friends. I will never let myself become a victim of alcohol." Now his addiction to alcohol has become notorious. While he is drunk, he raves and often uses abusive language. He has become a nuisance in the locality.

His drinking has disturbed his family life, too. Most of his income is consumed by liquor. As a result, he is left with a meagre amount to happy needs. His wife and children have to wear shabby clothes. Sometimes, he is unable to buy provisions for the month. Last month, his son's name was struck off the rolls of the school as he did not pay his school fees for several months. His wife did not like this development. She rebuked Manohar for neglecting the family and asked him to stop drinking. To silence her, he shouted and said: "Keep quiet or I will beat you to death." At this, she threatened to leave the house immediately. This was enough provocation for Manohar to beat her black and blue. Now his house is like a hell.

Manohar's case clearly shows that good habits take time to be cultivated while bad habits spring up like weeds. Carelessness in the matter of cultivating habits is just not harmful but sometimes it spells disaster also. Thus one should be fully alert in the matter of preventing the formation of bad habits.

Release Possible

If per chance one has contracted evil habits, it does not mean that he should put up with their tyranny throughout life. A friend of mine was a smoker for 15 years. Two years back, he said good-bye to smoking and has not touched the cursed stick again.

All habits depend upon self-discipline and self-denial. By developing these qualities, one can get rid of bad habits at any stage of life and can enjoy the sunshine of success and happiness. But wishing is not enough. One must know how to break a bad habit.

Ratan complains of pain and depression after meals. He has a disturbed sleep. He wears a gloomy look and feels irritated over trifles. Even in the company of friends, he feels like an odd man out. As for his work, he does all jobs in a slipshod manner.

His wife explains why Ratan feels gloomy. Ratan has appeared at the departmental examination thrice but has failed to qualify for promotion to a higher rank. He has now somehow convinced himself that success will not smile on him at all and he will have to stagnate as a section officer. Obsessed with the fear of a bleak future, he has lost interest in everything. At the dining table also, melancholy thoughts dominate his mind. He goes through meals hurriedly. Inevitably, he suffers from stomach trouble and other ailments.

The analysis of Ratan's case shows that he is a victim of bad emotional habits. He can get rid of the negative emotion of fear concerning his supposed bleak future by developing a mature outlook on life. He should know that he is holding his present job because he had some significant success in the past. There is no reason why his talent which in the past had brought him success will not do so in future. He should also remember that no one can wholly rule out some setback even when he is at the peak of his success. So one must learn to take some setbacks in one's stride. He should not let them throw him off the track.

This attitude towards life scares away all gloomy thoughts. Disappearance of gloomy thoughts cures many ills. If a person does not harbour gloomy thoughts while he is taking meals, he will get enough saliva to swallow the food. Food taken in this manner will be easily digested. Its reward will be sound sleep and freedom from pain and other irritating feelings.

Anita harbours no gloomy thoughts. Instead, she begins her work every day with tremendous gusto. Yet she feels exhausted very soon and finds herself unable to cope with the work. Her fault is that she chooses to do the easier tasks during the first half of the day and leaves the difficult ones for the second half. While she goes about her work, she knows no rest. Non-stop working leaves her completely exhausted before it is lunch time. It is not surprising if, she has little desire to tackle the difficult tasks during the second half. Result? Difficult tasks go on piling. When she thinks of her unfinished tasks, she feels much worried.

Anita's problems will disappear if she changes her habit. She should realize that if one works without interruption for many hours, it impairs one's capacity for work. There are only few people who can put in a long day and give as efficient service in the second half as they do in the first. The most efficient way is to work at intervals and to relax and rest inbetween.

Pre-planned Priorities

Tasks planned in order of priority also considerably improve one's efficiency. Difficult tasks should be accomplished during the first half of the day because at that time we have enormous energy which these tasks need. Easier tasks should be left to be tackled during the second half as they will need less energy. In this way, one can avoid the disappointment and worry resulting from unfinished tasks and enjoy the happiness which stems from accomplishing a task satisfactorily.

Bimla's problem is different from Anita's. Bimla wants to preserve her youthful vigour for ever. For this purpose, she excessively relies on tonics and other medicines. She thinks that medicines are an open sesame to radiant health. Even if she has a minor stomach trouble, her hand at once reaches out for the bottle of medicine. If you tell her that excessive dependence on medicine eventually wrecks health, she will reply, "What I take is a vegetable purgative." She does not seem to realize that these so-called vegetable purgatives and fruit salts prove highly detrimental if taken regularly. Their constant use causes irritation in the bowels and damages the delicate intestinal lining in the stomach. Very soon, one becomes a victim of chronic stomach trouble. Addiction to tonics is also equally harmful.

If a person really wants to enjoy sparkling health, he must abandon the medicine-taking habit. He should regulate his diet and avoid taking too much spices as they cause burning sensation in the stomach. A little regular exercise too should not be forgotten.

Your Personality is Your Fortune

To be successful, a person must know what makes people tick and know how to make them tick in the desired manner. A well-groomed personality does it all. You also know that personality is not wholly a divine gift. Your personality is largely what you make it.

Last week, I attended the birthday party of a friend's son. When the party was in progress, a large number of people swarmed around a gentleman like bees around a flower. As he was talking, they listened to him with rapt attention.

Obviously, his talk was absorbing. At this, one wondered if he possessed the power to hypnotize people. The truth was that he did not possess any such uncanny power. It was only the radiance of his magnetic personality which cast a spell over the invitees.

A grand personality is not something uncanny and unearthly. It is also not impossible to acquire. Personal magnetism is a divine spark which glows in all men and women. Some take care to develop this spark into a fine flame, while others let it burn dimly.

Obviously, the first type of people enjoy the sunshine of prestige and popularity and the second type are condemned to live in dark obscurity. One forms the group of celebrities, the other the mere crowd.

The term personality has a tremendous fascination for people. We often hear them say that Mr. X has a grand personality or that Miss Y has a poor personality. By this, they only mean a person's looks, voice, dress and manners. These external aspects are no doubt important, but they constitute only one factor.

Personality is a very comprehensive term. It includes many more things than mere externals. Allport, the noted psychologist, says, "Personality is the dynamic organisation within the individual of those psycho-physical systems that determine his unique adjustments to his environment."

Another psychologist, Dale Carnegie, says, "Personality is a vague and elusive thing defying analysis, like the perfume of a violet."

Personality may be complex and elusive to define. But it is not incapable of acquisition and perfection. Aldous Huxley says, "Every man who knows how to read has it in his power to magnify himself, to multiply the ways in which he exists, to make his life full, significant and interesting."

If you aspire to reach the peak in life and enjoy glory and esteem among your colleagues and fellows, you must first weave an excellent pattern of your personality. The way to do it is here.

No one can command respect from others unless he is successful in his work. To be successful is not an impossible thing. Anyone, regardless of his station in life, can become successful. The degree of success you enjoy will depend on how much effort you are willing to expend and how you approach the task.

Talent without the will to work is as useless as a boat without an oar. It is through work alone that we can demonstrate our intelligence and talent to others. Without such a demonstration, you cannot hope to reap any benefits. You may feel that you do not possess talent. Absurd, We all are endowed with a talent in varying degrees.

Formula of Success

What you have to do is to perfect that talent through application. For this, you must develop grit and patience.

You and Your Fortune

Fortune is painted blind, with a muffer afore her eyes, to signify to you that Fortune is blind, and she is painted also with a wheel, to signify to you, which is the moral of it, that she is turning and inconstant, and mutability and variation; and her foot, look you, is fixed upon a spherical stone which rolls and rolls and rolls.

—***Shakespeare***

A great fortune is a great slavery.

–*Seneca*

Fortune is like glass—the brighter the glitter, the more easily broken.

—*Publilius Syrus*

Efficiency in work does not come overnight. The path is sometimes rugged. If you receive jerks and jolts, you should not feel disheartened. It is just a test of your manhood, which you surely have in abundance in yourself.

You need to acquire professional competence and efficiency as it sets you apart from the crowd. But here, one pitfall should be avoided. It is the tendency to compare your achievements unfavourably with those of others. Such, comparison causes jealousy and frustration.

Remember, the person who is ahead of you today has behind him experience of several years. It is quite possible that your performance may be much better when you will have put in the same number of years in your job. Even otherwise, unfavourable comparison is not desirable.

Once, Rabindranath Tagore was asked if he considered Shakespeare a greater playwright than Kalidas. He said, "Art hates comparisons". In fact, no two persons are alike. I am I and you are you. Thus, our ways of working and achievements are bound to differ.

The important thing is that instead of comparing yourself with others, you should preserve and nourish the unique identity of your personality. The men who want to move the world and cover themselves with the halo of glory make conscious efforts to build their distinct personalities. Progress of modern civilization bears an eloquent testimony to this fact.

The way you should build your professional competence is this: Become your own rival. See that your performance today is better than what it was yesterday. If you improve yourself steadily day after day, after some time you will realize that your competence has surpassed your dream even. You know that no drop is insignificant in filling a pitcher.

Professional competence is no doubt very important. But the craze for professional competence has positive dangers too. Van Gogh's masterpieces are known and imitated throughout the world. Yet he committed suicide at the age of thirty-seven.

Frederic Chopin and Edgar Allan Poe were geniuses, had incredible professional ability, yet each died a miserably unhappy man. Why? They had neglected other vital traits of their personalities. So beware lest the competence mania should cause a similar split in your personality.

It is indisputable that professional competance plays a vital role in paving one's way to success. But it does not bring the desired success unless it is coupled with self-reliance.

Kuldip does not realize the importance of this vital truth. He blames circumstances and luck for his failure. To support his contention, he cites the case of Raman, who has been appointed a manager in a government undertaking because he had the recommendations of a minister. It is true that some persons are able to get profitable positions because of nepotism. But this does not prove the rule.

Hard Work

Most people pave their way to success through hard work. Success achieved in this way is a rest one, and fills you with genuine pride. Those who hold key positions undeservedly are like men with crutches who can only limp along but cannot run.

You know that even some physically handicapped persons who have self-respect in them refuse to seek charity. On the other hand, they learn certain skills to earn their living respectfully.

Surely Kuldip is not as poorly equipped as the physically handicapped. In fact, he is one of those whom success evades because they are reluctant to put in earnest efforts. Actually, only those get success who deserve it.

Ramesh is unlike Kuldip. He is quite successful in his professional life. But in social life, he ploughs a lonely furrow. Reason? He has no modesty. He always boasts of his achievements and speaks of others in a disparaging manner. Understandably, his popularity is at a low ebb. This unpleasant fact pinches Ramesh when he thinks of his colleague, Manohar.

Manohar is as successful in his professional life as Ramesh. But he does not boast before others. On the contrary, he is always ready to learn even from his subordinates. He admits candidly that he often gathers much valuable knowledge from his subordinates. He knows that no man is an island in himself. He buys knowledge with courtesy, as he knows that nothing costs less than courtesy.

People like Manohar make others feel easy, happy and bigger. They also are ever ready to help others. They can be fully relied upon in time of need. As there is no fear of fault-finding, you can discuss all your personal difficulties with them.

In the company of such a man, you open your heart, just as a flower opens to the sun. But in the company of a person like Ramesh, you feel unhappy, fearful and restless; you dare not discuss your problems with him. In fact, you have to wear a mask of reservation very tightly, just as you do your quilt in winter to prevent penetration of cold.

Another mark of a healthy personality is sobriety in dress, manners and speech. To make a good impression on others, it is not necessary that you should be very smartly dressed. No one likes a clown except for temporary amusement. Neat and sober dress is the universal hall-mark of a gentleman.

This principle applies to talk as well. Some people indulge in coarse and foul talk in order to make themselves the focus of other's attention. But actually, this is wrong. Coarse and foul talk can't give real pleasure. It sickens after a while. So you should cultivate the habit of clean, straight, strong talk. Any man, anywhere, anytime, will stop and listen to such talk.

The grooming of your personality is not complete yet. Your dress, manners and speech create only a first good impression. The first impression is not always the last impression, as some think. This is only a begginning. Promises, they say, win friends, but it is performance that keeps them. And performance needs sincerity.

If you do not redeem your promises and help people, they will very soon get disenchanted with you. Thus a first impression is not all. It is the real man that counts, the man inside the clothes, the man behind the smile.

To be successful, a person must know what makes people tick and know how to make them tick in the desired manner. A well-groomed personality does it all. You also know now that personality is not wholly a divine gift. Your personality is largely what you make it.

■■

What Enthusiasm Can do for You

Enthusiasm is a state of mind that determines our attitude towards life. It breeds optimism and an enthusiastic approach to life provides a man with powerful driving force.

You are not doomed to be a failure. Why should you, after all? If you wish to transform your dreams into reality, if you want to outshine others in your professional career, learn the secret of enthusiasm. The moment you have discovered this secret, success cannot elude you.

Enthusiasm is a state of mind that determines our attitude towards life. It makes the difference between living and just existing. An enthusiastic approach to life provides a man with a powerful driving-force. Difficulties and obstacles disappear from the path of an enthusiastic person just as ghosts flee before an enchanter.

Enthusiasm breeds optimism. An optimist always says to himself, "I can do it." But a pessimist says to himself, "I can't do it." Obviously, the former accomplishes any task he takes up in hand. The latter fails. One lives happily; the other is miserable.

Some persons perform their duties perfunctorily. They begin to suffer from feelings of exhaustion before they have finished half of the day's work.

Bimla is young and healthy. She has a maid-servant for domestic chores. The only task left for her is cooking meals for her small family comprising of her husband, two children and herself. But she takes even this as a burden.

Every day, after the preparation of lunch and dinner, she complains of exhaustion and stretches herself on the sofa, almost half dead. Her talk with her neighbours usually turns into a discourse on the difficulties of cooking.

Kamlesh, Bimla's neighbour, has just the opposite attitude towards work. For her, work is joy. She teaches in a school. She herself cooks for the family. She stitches garments for her children. Besides, she is preparing herself for the M.A. examination.

Inspite of all this, she never complains of weariness. The secret of her vitality is that she has learnt to mix enthusiasm with work.

Enthusiasm is contagious. An enthusiastic person changes the atmosphere of the place where he is present. His zeal points out the new possibilities of success in life to others. He does not brood over his past mistakes, insults and disappointments. He knows this cripples enthusiasm.

He is also fully aware that such irritants in life are inevitable. So he takes it easy. If you keep company with such a person, you will soon realize the difference. You will feel that you have come out of a dark, dingy room into an open, sunny place.

Enthusiasm without a goal to achieve is useless. Unharnessed enthusiasm turns into day-dreaming. Contemplation divorced from action bears no fruit. It only fosters the spirit of indolence. So always set some goal before you. Work earnestly to achieve it.

Remember, enthusiastic people are not magicians. They cannot accomplilsh all the tasks. In fact, they are the people who make a success of eight things out of ten. How does enthusiasm help them? Unenthusiastic people embark upon a plan with fond hopes of success. When they are confronted with difficulties, they abandon it in a huff. Thus, they never wear the crown of success. But enthusiastic people go through the hazards cheerfully and do not give up their plans until they reach completion

There is a man in my village who, 15 years ago, set up a small grocery store in a mud-plastered room. Everybody then thought he would just make a bare living with the income of the store. Nobody thought he would prosper.

For three or four years, he did not fare well. This seemed to confirm the villager's prediction. But Ram Chander did not wear a gloomy look. He did not complain to anyone of his not faring well. Whoever asked, he confidently told him that he was sailing smoothly.

The people hardly believed him. But a time came when his business showed a sudden spurt. He surprised everyone by installing a flour-mill and an oil-expeller. Now he owns a brick-kiln, two trucks and a leading grocery shop in the city.

Personal tragedies and crises tend to cause a temporary slump in enthusiasm. About ten years ago, a woman related to me first lost her husband and later her only son. She sank into despair. She became indifferent to all things. If a neighbour invited her on the occasion of her son's birthday, she herself stayed at home and perfunctorily sent the present through someone.

She dreaded the sight of any festivity. Most of the time, she confined herself to her house, brooding over the tragic past. When she continued living like this for some years, it seemed that she had lost all zest for life. But with the passage of time, her grief lost its sting and she realized that what had happened could not be undone.

She came out of the shell of isolation and adopted a son. He is now married and has children. She finds much pleasure in looking after her grand-children. She is so much devoted to her new family that the tragic past torments her no more.

Develop faith in yourself, and enthusiasm will bubble up in you. God has created man in his own image. Why not rely on the tremendous powers of the divinity in you?

If you distrust your ability, which is a divine gift, you distrust God. Faith moves mountains. Let it swing your mind and body into action. The rewards will surprise you. ■■

Youth is No Folly

Lives of all these great men lead us to the conclusion that success does not come to those who flirt with their youth and flout the spirit of disciplined work. Nor does it come by seeking charity from fate. Success woos a person if he learns to keep before him the following motto right from the early age: "Fruits of labour are sweeter than gifts of fortune."

Today, we find a large number of young people frittering away their precious energy and time in useless pursuits like drinking, smoking and addiction to narcotics. Young people indulge in such activities in the hope of deriving maximum enjoyment. But in the long run, they become disillusioned and frustrated.

True, youth is a time of enjoyment, because at this stage one has few worries. But youth is also the time of creative activity on which the excellent edifice of adulthood is built. Happy and prosperous adulthood is not possible if you flirt with your youth.

History is replete with examples of people who, by devoting themselves to creative activity in their young days not only covered themselves with glory but also bestowed numerous blessings on mankind.

SOS...SOS...This distress signal flashed across the Atlantic as Jack Phillips, wireless operator of the Titanic, told the world that the impossible had happened to the giant, unsinkable. White star ocean-liner was sinking on her maiden voyage. It had struck against a mountainous iceberg hidden by the Atlantic fog.

April 15, 1912 found 1500 people struggling for life in the ice-waters. Only 706 lived to tell of the horrible disaster. They owed their lives to one man, and when their rescue-ship reached New York, he was there to meet them. They shouted their thanks, "We owe our lives to you Marconi."

Wirelesss had won a great victory, and Marconi's struggle for recognition was over. Now, every time the radio delights our homes with heart-soothing music, we implicitly pay tributes to Marconi's greatness, who, by scorning delights and living laborious days in his youth, conferred this gift upon us.

At twelve, Marconi became interested in physics, chemistry and electrical research. At fifteen, as a student of the University of Bologna, he first read of the wireless waves which could span the earth, and he felt the urge to explore their use as a means of rapid communication.

At twenty-one, Marconi started on his life's project, whose accomplishment involved a number of difficulties. But undaunted, he pursued his goal. His new equipment complete, twenty-two-year-old Marconi received quick recognition by big business companies and the Government of Britain.

Thomas Edison, the great inventor, equally owed his achievements to the diligence he displayed in his youth. Edison had developed a very inquisitive mind, and was always asking, "Why am I here?" This showed his burning desire to unravel the secrets of nature for the benefit of his fellow-beings.

At the age of six, he set fire to his father's barn just to see what would happen. The barn burnt to the ground and Thomas also got burnt with it. But this did not dampen his inquisitive spirit. In fact, he was so eager to learn from every source that he approached even strangers without any hesitation answers to his questions.

At the age of ten, when most boys read adventure stories or comics, he read serious books on chemistry. At 15, he became editor and publisher of the Weekly Herald. In short, he fully realised the significance of creative living at an early age.

He had cultivated such a zest for living that he considered waste of even a single minute as criminal. This is why he was able to make innumerable inventions whose significance we cannot forget in our daily life even for a while.

As long as we listen to recorded music, get pleasure in a cinema house, travel in comfort in an electric train or read with the aid of an electric lamp, we are using a gift given to us by Edison.

President Kennedy was not only a brilliant statesman but also a brilliant student. He graduated from the Harvard University in 1940 with top grades in political science. At twenty-three, he won fame for his book, "Why England Slept."

The name of Raja Ram Mohan Roy is recalled with great reverence as the father of Indian Renaissance. He laid the foundations of several movements that were calculated to lead India on to the path of progress. He was able to initiate social and religious reforms, like abolition of Sati and exposing the hypocrisy of priestcraft through the Brahmo Samaj, because at an early age, he had developed an enlightened mind.

As a young man, he assiduously studied Sanskrit, Persian, Arabic and scriptures, which developed in him a keen power of discrimination about social and religious values.

Tilak was also aware of the dangers of neglecting the youthful days. At an early age, he became seriously engrossed in studies. At the age of ten, he acquired a nodding acquaintance with the works of Kalidasa, Bhavbhuti, Dandi and Bharavi.

He never shirked hard work. This is beautifully illustrated by an incident which occurred in his life when he was just a child. One day, Tilak's father was engrossed in unravelling the word combinations of Kadambri, a great Sanskrit play written by Bana. Per chance, Tilak was playing around.

Tilak demanded the book his father was reading.

To put him off, his father said that he could get the book on the condition of solving a sum in arithmetic. Tilak agreed, and a fairly difficult sum was set to him. He found it pretty difficult, but did not grumble.

After struggling for two hours, he solved it. Exhilerated by his success, he demanded Kadambri, and his father had to surrender. The secret of Tilak's success in later life was that he brought to bear on every situation the same intellectual powers, courage, resolution and absorption. He counted no effort too arduous for a cause.

Success was Gokhale's ally, because at an early age, he had begun to look upon hard work as a sacred ritual to be performed every day. No wonder his short span of life was crowded with great achievements. He became a graduate at 18, a professor and associate editor of the Sadharak at 20, editor of the Quarterly Journal and the Secretary of the Sarvjanik Sabha at 21, Secretary of the Bombay Provincial Conference at 25, Secretary of the Indian National Congress at 34, President of the Indian National Congress at 39.

Was Gokhale, whom Gandhiji regarded as his political Guru, a minion of fortune? Certainly not. He had ample taste of hardships and rigours of life. He was able to fill his short span of life with services of such magnitude and splendour because of his dedication and idealism—a vision of life he had conjured up in his early youth.

New Era

Jules Verne ushered in a new era through his scientific-fiction writing. What a great source of inspiration his writings are to explorers and scientists can be gauged from the following remarks: "Modern scientists are simply putting into practice what Verne had conceived so clearly and described so vividly in his books. They are turning his fancy into fact."

No doubt, Jules was endowed with a great intellectual gift. But to make his talent bear fruit, he needed training. He equipped himself with this training by slogging a lot in his youth. In God's plan, opportunity always comes to those who have done their part of the project by careful planning and adequate preparation. Jules Verne got this opportunity which catapulted him into prominence and prosperity.

Leonardo da Vinci, whose paintings cast a spell over people throughout the world, began to display his unique talent and love of hard work at an early age. At fifteen, he was an avid collector of insect specimens.

His talent, coupled with hard work, blossomed into excellent paintings which earned him a niche in the galaxy of great artists.

Pascal died at 39. But he had already been made immortal by his scientific inventions. Fame first came to him because he invented the calculating machine which relieved people working in offices of the drudgery of calculating. Apart from this, modern computors, airplanes, altimetres, hydraulic devices, we primarily owe to Pascal's scientific thinking.

A cursory look at Pascal's life will reveal how he had begun to value hard work in his young days. At 12, he was busy working with mathematical diagrams. In this way, he was trying to discover the principles of geometry. At 16, he wrote an important essay on Conics—a mathematical topic.

Lavoisier, whose discoveries have revolutionised chemistry, was a very diligent student. By the time he was 25, he had won an award for a plan to improve the lighting of the streets of Paris. Besides, he became a member of the French Academy of Sciences. He was able to win these laurels because he learned stern intellectual discipline from his teacher, who was a hard taskmaster.

J.S. Mill, too, learned the value of careful planning and perseverance early in life. At 18, he was given the task of editing Bentham's Rationale of Judicial Evidence.

Karl Marx, whose political philosophy has exercised enormous influence on people in modern times, realised early in life that hard work was an open sesame to success in life.

At 19, he had translated large parts of Tecitus and Ovid and prepared a work of three hundred pages on the philosophy of law. While out of sorts, he learnt Hegel from beginning to end!

Man of the Moon

Neil Armstrong was acclaimed as a great hero all over the world when he became the first man to land on the moon. Fate did not offer him success on a silver platter. Success came to him because he had already perspired a lot in his job.

It is instructive to know the steps Neil Armstrong followed to climb the ladder of success. At six, he accompanied his father for his first airplane ride. Then he made the first model airplane. Hundreds more followed, till he felt satisfied.

He had no time for comics. He devoured books and magazines on aviation. He read ninety books during his first year in school, and so jumped the next class. At 17, he studied aeronautical engineering at the university.

Lives of al these great men lead us to the conclusion that success does not come to those who flirt with their youth and flout the spirit of disciplined work. Nor does it come by seeking charity from fate. Success woos a person if he learns to keep before him the following motto right from the early age: "Fruits of labour are sweeter than gifts of fortune."

Don't Foster an Emotional Scar

Life is a great adventure in which we are likely to receive hard knocks. But we should not let jolts fill us with shattering gloom. On the other hand, when confronted with unfavourable situations, we should display a sportsman like attitude.

Twenty-one-year-old Usha one day fell down while trying to ride an over-crowded bus and received a serious injury on the face. As a result of medical treatment, the injury has been cured, but a black scar has developed on her face.

Several women in the neighbourhood tell Usha's mother that the scar on her daughter's face will affect her marital prospects. When young and sensitive Usha hears these words, she feels quite nervous and unhappy. These thoughts also sometimes distract her mind from her studies.

If Usha allows these negative thoughts to tenant her mind, soon they will cause an emotional bruise and become a kill-joy for her. Usha should realise that the scar on her face does not bear testimony to any evil deed of which she should feel ashamed. Moreover, the scar can't eclipse her other good qualities for marital purposes.

If anyone refuses to marry her only because of this reason, it is not desirable to have such a partner at all. After all, no young man likes to be rejected by his prospective bride if per chance he has developed some physical defects. Thus, it is wise to avoid cultivating an emotional scar, as it can play havoc with your happiness and success.

History is replete with examples of persons who did not let their afflictions develop into emotional scars and imperil their success and happines. Helen Keller became blind, deaf and mute quite early in life. But she did not let her handicaps develop into a hurdle. Impelled by her valiant spirit, she overcame all the impediments in her way.

Under the inspiring guidance of her teacher, Sullivan, she learnt English, Latin, French and German. By writing books like: *The Story of My Life, The World I Live In, Let Us Have Faith,* etc. she made a significant contribution to literature.

She was not content to engage herself in intellectual pursuits only. She had a very compassionate heart. When World War II broke out, she visited hospitals and brought comfort to hundreds of wounded men. She shared no effort to make the lives of the afflicted richer and happier.

Eulogising Helen Keller's passion to relieve sufferings of her fellow-beings, President Eisenhower wrote to her, "The Story of your accomplishment is not only the monument to your great gift of mind and heart, it is also an enduring inspiration to many lands... to those who have suffered physical handicaps and to those who seek to help the disabled towards richer lives."

Maharaja Ranjit Singh was illiterate and blind in one eye. But he did not allow these obstructions to bar his way to success. His unique achievement was that he carved out a powerful and efficiently administered Sikh state out of the numerous feuding factions and principalities.

As long as Ranjit Singh was alive, the British Government did not dare to cast its covetous eyes on his kingdom, as they had done in the case of many other native states.

From this you need not jump to the conclusion that only great persons are capable of enjoying happiness and success in life despite their severe foibles. Lesser mortals too, with their courage and endurance, can transform their misfortunes into happiness and success.

Shanti lost her husband over thirty years ago. Six months after her husband's demise, her five-year-old son too passed away. She was only twenty-five when these heart-rending tragedies struck her.

Swaran was married to an officer in the Indian Air Force. As her husband was kind and considerate, she enjoyed conjugal happiness abundantly. She also enjoyed a sophisticated social life—visiting clubs, giving and attending parties. The birth of a son seemed to complete Swaran's happiness. Her son was only two years old when war broke out between India and Pakistan in 1971, and her husband valiantly laid down his life defending his country.

This was clearly a shattering blow to Swaran's happiness. Her plight was now like that of a charming flower which, torn off the stem by a violent storm, was lying in the dust. To regain her happiness, one alternative before her was to re-marry and set up a new home.

As she was much devoted to her husband, she did not entertain any idea of remarriage. She decided to be self-reliant and bring up her son. Before marriage, she had done her B.A., which now stood her in good stead. She underwent teacher's training and joined a girl's school as a teacher.

Though her present life implies genial of several comforts and pleasures which she enjoyed when her husband was alive, she is fully reconciled to her lot and finds her job and the task of rearing her son quite satisfying.

My friend, Hari Sharkar's wife, died of an ailment three years ago. The tragedy, apart from causing deep sorrow, placed on his shoulders the responsibility of looking after his three children single-handed. Instead of rushing himself into the morass of unnecessary sorrow, cursing fate for treating him shabbily, he took a pragmatic view of the situation.

He took special care to cater to the needs of his children, so that they might not feel the void caused by the death of their mother. To save himself from the deleterious impact of sorrow, he started his Ph.D. and completed it within two years. Thus he converted his loss into gain.

Life is a great adventure in which we are likely to receive

hard knocks. But we should not let jolts fill us with shattering gloom. On the other hand, when confronted with unfavourable situations, we should display a sportsman-like attitude. The Nawab of Pataudi lost his one eye while playing a cricket match. But this did not wear him away from cricket. In fact, his zeal for the game continues unabated as ever.

Dr. Joseph Murphy rightly observes, "If you really want peace of mind and inner calm, you will get it. Regardless how unjustly you have been treated or how unfair the boss has been or what a mean scoundrel someone has proved to be, all this makes no differences to you when you awaken to your mental and spiritual powers.

You know what you want and you will definitely refuse to let the thieves (thoughts) of hatred, anger, hostility and ill-will rob you of peace, harmony, health and happiness."

He goes on, "You cease to become upset by people, conditions, news and events by identifying your thoughts immediately with your aim in life."

■■

Why Great Men are Great

Real greatness springs from contribution one makes for promoting the welfare of his fellow-beings. Greatness is the perfume of good ideas and virtuous deeds.

Greatness does not emanate from acquisition of power or amassing of wealth for self-aggrandisement. Real greatness springs from the contribution one makes for promoting the welfare of his fellow-beings. In short, greatness is the perfume of good ideas and virtuous deeds. Glimpses of great men's personalities beautifully illustrate this fact.

Deniel Defoe's *A Journal of the Plague Year* published from London in 1772 records horrors of smallpox thus: 'The shrieks of the women and children at the windows and doors of their houses, where their dearest relations were dying or just dead were so frequently to be heard that it was enough to pierce the stoutest hearts in the world to hear them.' All the countries of the world were vulnerable to this

> **As the teacher, so the student**
>
> Writing in the American journal *National Parent-Teacher*, an American critic defines current education as 'that mysterious process whereby information passes from the lecture notes of the professor, throught the fountain pen and on the note-book of the student, without passing through the mind of either.'

scourge of smallpox and felt powerless to do anything when afflicted.

Edward Jenner discovered a vaccination whose inoculation made people completely invulnerable to smallpox. If Jenner wanted he could have minted money by keeping the secret of vaccination to himself. But his magnanimous heart could not allow such a desire to overwhelm him.

Joseph Farington records in his famous diary that when Sir Walter Farquhar made this suggestion to Jenner that he could earn £ 10,000 a year by preserving this secret, he at once turned it down. He published his discovery in 1798 for the benefit of all mankind.

Money never attracted him. His sole aim was to serve humanity. Small wonder nearly three hundred poor patients waited at his door everyday to be vaccinated free of charge.

Albert Einstein, who won unique fame in the realm of science because of his *'Theory of Relativity'* also wanted his scientific talent to be used to bring peace and prosperity to his fellow-beings. In 1914 he was a professor at the Prussian Academy of Sciences. When the German government asked him to use his special scientific talent to aid the war effort he refused bluntly. He said, 'This war is a vicious and savage crime. I would rather be hacked to pieces than take part in such an abominable business.' On another occasion he said, 'I am absolutely convinced that no wealth in the world can help humanity forward. The world needs permanent peace and lasting goodwill.'

Einstein's modesty was as amazing as his scientific brilliance. Once the Queen of Belgium invited him and sent for him a limousine to the railway station. Einstein without informing the reception staff walked to the place in his ill-tailored suit, carrying his violin with him. When the Queen asked him why he had not used the limousine he just said, 'It was a very pleasant walk, your Majesty.' His brilliant mind coupled with a compassionate heart and humility made him immortal.

Guru Nanak is one of the most remarkable personages of all times who tried to relieve the distress of his fellow-beings. He launched a crusade to debunk religious dogmatism and break down caste-barriers which served as a drag on people's progress and exposed them to the evils like avarice, communal rancour and superstition.

To worldly farmers he gave the advice, 'Make the body the field, good works the seed, irrigate with God's name.' To those who made pilgrimages for show he said, 'What availeth it to bathe at a place of pilgrimage if the filth of pride be in the heart.' To preach his message of universal brotherhood he visited Persia, Arabia and China.

The era in which Confucius was born in China was virtually a living inferno because of rampant exploitation of masses by feudal lords. Through his teachings he gave a new vision to his countrymen and made vigorous efforts to purge the society of prevalent stink. He attached paramount importance to hardwork and denounced slothfulness.

As for the form of government he did not insist on strict conformity and stifling dissent. He said, 'The right to govern depends upon the ability to make the governed happy and secure.' On international relations too his views are refreshingly modern. Realising the importance of co-existence among different nations of the world he said, 'Aggression by any state or nation should be outlawed.'

Like Confucius, Henry David Thoreau was also a man of great vision and humanism. Thoreau's ideas have exercised enormous influence throughout the world. Both Mahatma Gandhi and Martin Luther King, a noted American Negro leader, came under his spell. Thoreau despised ostentatious life and conspicuous consumption. To lead a life of strict austerity he lived at the Walden Pond away from the glitter of urban life. Likewise Mahatma Gandhi Lived at Sabarmati, a small village far away from the din and glamour of city-life

Thoreau also strongly pleaded for resisting political tyranny. He said: 'Unjust laws exist: shall we be content to obey them or shall we transgress them at once? If unjust laws exist civil disobedience is an effective way to oppose and change them. There will never be a really free and enlightened State until the State comes to recognise the individual as a higher and independent power; from which all its power and authority are derived and treats him accordingly.'

Mahatma Gandhi derived great inspiration from Thoreau's concept of civil disobedience and used this weapon with amazing efficacy to fight the tyranny of British imperialism.

Are You Unconventional?

Unconventional thinking pays rich dividends and is the key to progress.

Man's landing on the moon has in a way shown the triumph of free-thinking. The process whose grand culmination we have witnessed now in the form of the conquest of the moon began six hundred years ago. At that time science was handmaid of the Church. If anyone tried to question the validity of the scientific observations made by the classical writers he was treated as a heretic. His observations were declared to be inspired by the devil. If any scientist showed courage of conviction there was every possibility of his being put to death. Fresh thinking was forbidden not only in scientific enquiry but in all intellectual activity.

But there were some intellectuals who undaunted by the threat of severest penalties recorded their independent views and propagated them. Modern civilization of which we are so proud has been made possible by the courage, determination and sacrifices of these great men.

Copernicus was one such person who had made unconventional scientific observations. Like all others he started teaching astronomy according to the Ptolemaic laws at the University of Rome. This theory placed the earth in the centre of the universe and the sun and the stars as satellites that moved round the earth. When Copernicus appeared on the scene this system had already held sway for fifteen hundred years. There was not the slightest possibility of its being challenged.

But Copernicus soon became dissatisfied with the validity of the Ptolemaic theory. He recorded his independent views on the movement of planets. He declared that the earth moves round the sun. His uncommon observation provoked the wrath of his adversaries. They hired a number of clowns to burlesque his astronomical studies. But their ridicule did not affect the value of his observations.

Galileo was another great intellectual whose unconventional observations had made a significant contribution to scientific activity. Galileo's father sent him to study medicine at the University of Pisa. But he secretly studied mathematical works of Euclid and Archimedes. In his spare moments he conducted experiments with instruments he had made himself.

His professors soon got wind of his studies and experiments. They disapproved of them. In their opinion it was nothing short of a heresy for a student to think independently. All scientific problems, the professors declared, had been finally and conclusively settled by Aristotle. Whenever a student dared to raise an objection to a dogmatic pronouncement, the professors would settle the argument with a citation from Aristotle: Magister dixit, 'the Master has spoken'.

Galileo's unconventional thinking, his professors feared, would spoil the name of the university. They complained to his father. Galileo's father warned him to stop his objectionable activities. But he disregarded the warning. The professors refused to give him his doctor's diploma. So he left the University of Pisa—a failure in medicine and a 'crackbrained juggler of useless figures'.

At that time the study of mathematics was not popular. So Galileo could hardly find any pupil to maintain himself. But the heavy odds did not damp his passion for mathematical studies.

After he had conducted a series of experiments, contrary

to the teachings of Aristotle, he asserted that two different weights released simultaneously from the same height would fall to the ground at the same time. 'Nobody but a fool can believe that the feather and a cannon ball will travel downward through space at the same speed,' remarked his opponents.

In the midst of jeering crowds Galileo went up the leaning Tower of Pisa and simultaneously dropped two balls—one of ten pounds in weight and another one pound. To the utter surprise of his spectators both the balls hit the ground simultaneously. The event significant as it was, rudely jolted the ignorance of his detractors.

In the past, rigidity in thinking had not blocked the progress of science alone. In social and religious fields too it had bred a variety of evils. Here also nonconformists played a notable role.

Early years of the 16th century were a period of religious decadence. People all over Europe were disgusted with the behaviour of the priests. The cause of disgust was the notorious practice of Indulgences practised by the priests.

According to this theory the temporal punishment due for sin could be remitted in whole or part, in the case of those who, after confessing and showing contrition for their sins, received holy communion and performed some act of penance. In course of time the most popular act of penance became one of making a contribution to the temporal needs of the Church. In the hands of unscrupulous ecclesiastics the practice developed into a ready-money transaction.

Martin Luther, who was later known as the founder of Protestantism, raised his voice against the sale of Indulgences. He urged the people to stop purchasing Indulgences. He publicly exposed the evil motives of the priests behind the sale of Indulgences.

Luther's activities provoked the wrath of the Pope of Rome against him. The Pope issued an edict denouncing Luther's opinions. If Luther did not retract within sixty days he would be excommunicated, said the edict. Luther replied in an unusual way by burning a copy of the edict. The papal supremacy had been defied. The Reformation was launched. People reaped the benefit as the ecclesiastical order following this movement was largely purged of irreligious elements.

In our country Gandhiji was a great nonconformist in religious and social matters. It is because of his commendable efforts that the evil of untouchablity, though not fully eradicted, has lost much of its sting. Before Gandhiji, Ram Mohan Roy's heroic efforts has put an end to the monstrous practice of Sati. Similarly Ishwar Chandra Vidya Sagar by his powerful advocacy of widow-remarriage tried to remove the stigma attached to it and thus paved the way for female emancipation. Such efforts of these great men in those days when sterile orthodoxy was held sway, did not evoke praise. Instead, they were threatened with dire consequences for propagating their progressive views. Unmindful of threats to their lives they pursued their goals unswervingly. This is why our society is no longer plagued with these evils.

From this, one can easily infer that nonconformity pays rich dividends. The principle of nonconformity, good as it is, gets perverted into the hands of self-seekers. For instance, fast changing political loyalties to secure personal benefits reduce parliamentary democracy to a farce.

Nonconformity brings home to us the important point that values of life do not become worth preserving simply because they are rooted in antiquity. Nor should we assume that all observations and ideas of great men are infallible. Even Aristotle's observations were found fallible by Galileo.

The need today is to encourage fresh-thinking in our country on all important matters. Difference of opinion should not be interpreted as defiance of authority. If the intellectuals of the past had followed authority blindly, dazzling achievements of modern times would not have been possible.

Make Your Mind Behave

Good habits vitalize the mind and thus help in acquiring the power of concentration.

Kamla is a secretary in a business concern. One day her boss gave her an urgent letter to type. Within an hour she typed the letter. But when she placed it before her boss he began to rebuke her instead of saying 'well done'. Why? The letter was dotted with numerous typing errors which the boss found unpalatable. This is not a solitary case with Kamla. The sloppy habits of work have cost her two jobs before. In her present job too she has been stagnating for several years without getting any promotion.

But it is different with 16 year old Mohini. Recently she participated in an essay competition. Within an hour, the time allowed to all participants, she produced an excellent stuff. Her attempt was adjudged the best and she bagged the first prize.

You may say that Mohini won the first prize because of her superior intelligence. Yes, you are right. But there is something more than that.

And it is concentration. Without concentration intelligence cannot yield the desired results. In fact intelligence not coupled with concentration is as useless as beads without a thread. To derive the maximum pleasure the beads must be woven into a rosary which is possible only with a thread. Similarly to enjoy full benefits of intelligence one must make it an ally of concentration—a fact which Kamala had not understood. If Kamla acquired the power of concentration, she could avoid making mistakes. Like Mohini she too could earn praise instead of rebukes.

What is concentration? Nepoleon Hill defines concentration in his inspiring book 'the Law of Success' as follows: 'Concentration is the act of focusing the mind upon a given desire until ways and means for its realization have been worked out and successfully put into operation.'

In cultivating concentration two things play a vital role. These are habit and memory. Habit as you know is an act of doing the same thing in the same way over and over again. Habit grows out of environment. If you live in a healthy environment, you will develop healthy habits. If you live in an unhealthy environment, you contract bad habits. Good habits vitalize the mind and thus help in acquiring the power of concentration. Bad habits sap the energy and cause mental strain. Thus they block the way.

Remember, your environment is largely what you make it. If you choose to keep company with gamblers, drunkards, back-biters and the like, you cannot avoid cultivating bad habits. But if you keep company with persons engaged in creative work, corroding thoughts will never enter your mind. In such an atmosphere your mind will remain free from crippling distractions and the door to good habits will be unlocked easily for you.

A psychologist stresses the importance of habit in this manner "All men are creatures of habit and that habit is a cable; we weave a thread of it each day and it becomes so strong that we cannot break it." As habits die hard so one should take care not to let evil habits tenant the mind.

Memory is as essential an aid to concentration as habit. Memory has three characteristics-retention, recall and recognition. If you learn a thing today and forget it the following day, its advantages are clearly negligible for you. To retain a thing in your mind you should act like a lover. A lover is capable of retaining in his mind every impression of his beloved features and even the tone of her voice because of his keen interest in her. If you display the same interest in learning a thing, it will not slip out of your mind easily. Another thing is that it is not always possible that you will get the opportunity to use the learned thing the next day. Sometimes days and even months pass before you are able to use it. When the opportunity to use the learned material comes, you find yourself unable to recall it. Sometimes you succeed in recalling also but you are not sure that it is the same thing which you had learned. All these handicaps of memory can be overcome by developing keen interest and discrimination in learning a thing.

To develop interest and power of discrimination you can adopt the following methods. First, convince yourself that the thing you are planning to learn is of vital importance in improving your social and professional status. Such a conviction will take irk out of your work and your mind will absorb the material you want to learn with perfect ease. Second, you should not attempt to mug up all the material available on the topic. Instead, you should sift the important things out of the vast mass of information at your disposal. Then you should proceed to learn them in order of priority. Remember no one can learn all the things. To derive the maximum benefit you will do well to digest a few important facts rather than burden your mind with a mass of jumbled-up facts.

Ramesh swears that he is keenly interested in his studies. But as soon as he settles down to work, he says, his mind begins to wander. He further adds that sometimes after reading several pages of his book he finds he has not grasped anything. This problem is not peculiar to Ramesh. Many adolescents and even adults face this problem. The difficulty with such persons is that they allow their attention to be attracted by another task before they have finished the one in hand. The result is that they hardly succeed in achieving anything worthwhile. Persons like Ramesh obviously do not realize the truth that it is unwise to keep too many irons into the fire at a time.

Carlyle points out the futility of starting another work without finishing the one you have in hand in these words:

'The weakest creature by concentrating his powers on single object can accomplish something whereas the strongest by dispersing his over many may fail to accomplish anything.'

Indeed all great works of art and literature are fruits of concentration which their creators brought to bear on their work. In other words we can say that they could not realize their ambitions without concentration. Surely you are not without ambition. You also want to reap rich rewards with minimum effort. Concentration can do this all for you. This is by no means a tall claim. Charles Dickens, the famous Victorian novelist, owes his spectacular achievements to the power of concentration. He describes in the following words how the miraculous power of concentration proved beneficial to him: 'The one serviceable, safe, certain, remunerative, attainable quality in every study and pursuit is that of attention. My own imagination would never have served me as it did but for the habit of humble daily toiling attention.'

To acquire this power start your efforts now. Tomorrow may be late.

You Can Hit the Target

Don't get discouraged; it is often the last key in the bunch that opens the lock.

Most young people are fired by high ambitions in life. They wish to climb the dizzy heights of success. But many of them don't have a clear vision of the eventual goal they wish to attain. On the other hand they have a nebulous concept of aims they are seeking to achieve. Such persons may be like drivers of fast moving vehicles on an unfamiliar road on an intensely foggy day. Both the factors—lack of intimate knowledge of the way and poor visibility due to bad weather are likely to lead them astray. Similarly people with a hazy view of life are likely to miss their destination in life.

C. Harry Brooks aptly observes, "We are incapable of exercising the will unless the imagination has first furnished it with a goal. We cannot simply will, we must will something."

I recall the case of a youngman named Mohan whom success eluded as he had no specific target to shoot at. Mohan had both talent and youthful spirits wich are essential ingredients of success. First of all he set up a shop dealing in automobile spare parts. He expected a windfall in profits. Obviously he did not take into account the competition he would have to face from other dealers in the market. Soon realities began to assert themselves. Customers did not flock to his shop spell-bound as he had expected. Mohan had not developed the grit required to tide over this unpleasant phase which is inevitable in all enterprises. Disillusioned, he threw up his hands in despair and decided to wind up his business. He incurred a considerable loss.

Disenchantment with the automobile business induced him to set his heart on setting up a medical store at a vantage point in the city. He embarked upon his new venture with a lot of fanfare. After sometime when Mohan began to face some problems in this new project also, he began to curse fate instead of thinking of ways and means to solve them. Clearly he wanted fate to offer him success on a silver platter. He was not prepared to wrest it by the sweat of his brow. Unable to find a magic wand to overcome his difficulties he again succumbed to despair. He allowed difficulties to overwhelm him and, as a way out, he once again closed down.

Persons like Mohan who hop from one job to another without making a determined bid to succeed never cover themselves with glory. To woo the deity of success, a person has first of all to have a clear blueprint of his dream and then pursue it with grim resolve to make it come true. It is worthwhile to bear in mind that a beautiful building, the sight of which leaves us spell-bound has required digging in the mud and working in the scorching heat of the sun to lay its foundations and to raise its superstructure.

No youngman worth his salt allows himself to be daunted by the initial difficulties. He is fully aware that when a person cowed down by difficulties is about to quit, success is usually round the corner. Quitters will do well to profit by Trotty Veck's following sane counsel, "Don't get discouraged; it is often the last key in the bunch that opens the lock". W.T. Grenfell also endorses this view when he remarks, "Heroism is endurance for one moment more".

Sometimes, a young person is cheated of success not because he lacks grit but because he allows others to determine the goal for him. One who rows the boat of life in the direction determined by others often lands himself in trouble. It is worthwhile to point out that a vegetarian at a party will never take non-vegetarian dishes, however sumptuous they are. Similarly a teetotaller will never take liquor even if fullthroated praise is lavished on the pleasures of drinking. Fixing your goal in life is of vital importance. That determines whether a person will enjoy happiness or be condemned to frustration. One should make an objective assessment of one's assets and liabilities, tastes and distastes and then decide the destination one wants to reach. Like borrowed garments, life's goal if determined by others rarely paves the way to happiness.

True, utmost care is needed to determine the right goal for life. But to invest your dream with substance conscientious efforts play no less vital a role. At every step you have to be alert to eliminate slipshod work ruthlessly. A sculptor succeeds in making a beautiful statue out of a rough marble slab only when he does not brook the sligtest sloppiness in his working. Leonardo da Vinci's *Mona Lisa*, which evokes boundless admiration from art-lovers all over the world, is the fruit of a long-sustained, painstaking, patient effort. Those who have reached the top in their chosen field never considered any price too great to pay. They were fully aware that their product would proclaim the quality of their talent. And it is the quality of the work that draws a dividing line between failure and success.

Extolling the significance of meticulous effort, Orison Swett Marden says, "If you put your conscience into your work, the world will make a path to your door, though you live in the wilderness". William Mathews also casts his vote in Swett Marden's favour by observing, "A great deal of the joy of life consists in doing whatever you take up perfectly or at least to the best of your ability."

How to Capitalize on Your Mistakes

All the trouble in the world cannot sink a human being unless those troubles invade his inner life. Success comes to a person who has learnt to take all the jerks and jolts in his stride.

To err is human, goes the old saying. The wisdom enshrined in this proverb tells us that we should not feel discouraged if we are unable to achieve success in a single attempt. To expect instant success is to invite frustration.

Prem had an ambition to get an administrative job under the Government. To realise his ambition he started preparing for a competitive exam which was a few months away. He had ample time for preparation. He was very enthusiastic about getting the job. He had been a brilliant student and had earned high grades in all his university exams. It appeared to him that success was round the corner. He did reasonably well at the examination.

After some time, when the result was declared, he was shocked not to find his name on the list of successful candidates. This had a shattering effect on his mind. Filled with gloom which was writ large over his face, he went about cursing his fate for depriving him of his due reward. Not only that, he determined not to appear in any competitive examination in future.

Prem's friend Avinash too had apeared at the examination along with him. He too had done his papers well and hoped to qualify. Like Prem he too was unsuccessful. No doubt Avinash felt unhappy over his failure but he did not let his failure affect his thinking. His disappointment lasted only a few days, and then he regained his equanimity. He began preparing afresh with greater vigour. Per chance, success eluded him the next year also. Naturally Avinash felt disappointed. But he did not give up. He appeared in the examination for the third time. Happily, that time his efforts were crowned with success. Today Avinash basks in the glory and prestige that go with an administrative post. Prem, on the contrary remains a lacklustre plodder. The secret of Avinash's success is that he did not yield when failure struck twice. He was sincerely in love with his ambition, and wanted to make his dream come true at all costs. Eventually he was able to realise it.

Success comes to a person who has learnt to take all the jerks and jolts in his stride. Commenting on the significance of retainig one's poise, a writer has observed, "All the trouble in the world cannot sink a human being unless those troubles invade his inner life."

Evidently those who want to go up the ladder of success cannot afford to be afraid of making mistakes. They know that instant success is nothing but wishful thinking. They look upon mistakes as stepping stones to success. Keats' poems today are considered examples of perfection in romantic poetry. The muse did not offer these poems to Keats on a silver platter. He composed them, revised them and chiselled them again and again until they became archetypes of perfection. This leads us to the conclusion that excellence is the outcome of trial and error. In other words, mistakes have great educative value. If we have made a mistake, we should admit it and make all possible efforts to rectify it. We sould take steps to see that it is not repeated. That sort of attitude develops in us the faculty of discrimination which is the key to success. J.S. Mursel rigtly observes, "The number of times you try is not the important consideration. The important consideration is the intelligence with which you try and above all what you yourself discover from your mistakes."

Persistence is the key to success in any and every sphere. Names of persons like Jagadish Chandra Bose and C.V.Raman conjure up thrilling and heart-warming visions of success in the scientific firmament. They did not succeed in propounding their unique scientific theories in a single attempt. As a matter of fact they achieved dazzling fame because they were never afraid of making mistakes and learning from them. They had imbibed the significance of the dictum, "It is never too late to mend."

The path of success like the path of true love rarely run smooth. It is usually bumpy and rugged. On a bumpy road at times you are likely to slip despite your wary walking. On such occasions your adversaries may poke fun at you and do everything to discourage you. But a man of prudence never lets his detractors have the last laugh. Like an expert driver, he carefully handles the bumps on the road of life, and undaunted by the prophets of doom, he perseveres in his endeavours and eventually steals the show.

We should not dread failure. It is not a bad thing. In fact it is blessing in disguise. It plays a vital role in building and strengthening our character. One who has suffered bruises on the road of life is never callous or cruel. He never scoffs at others' mistakes. On the contrary, he contributes to others' success by showing sympathy and understanding. Our mistakes develop in us courage which is one of the crucial props of success. A man who has gone through the process of making mistakes and rectifying them develops endurance. He never expects that success will come to him just sitting pretty. Like a farmer he goes out to sweat in the scorching heat of the sun and is prepared to put up with the vagaries of rain and wind with confidence and courage, to be rewarded in the end with a plentiful harvest.

Tact Triumphs Over Talent

Tact is no substitute for talent; it is a life-belt without which many talents may well flounder

Talent may enable an engineer to manufacture an excellent machine. But that is not enough if he wants to convert his talent into cash. To get customers to patronise his product, he needs tact in ample measure. Without tact, talent is virtually useless like a record without a record-player. Lady Violet Bonham Carter rightly comments, "Tact is no substitute for talent; it is a life-belt without which many talents may well flounder".

Tact is skill in overcoming opposition and making other people eager to do what you want. The following example will illustrate how a ticklish problem can be easily solved with the help of tact. Once in the court of a judge, two ladies appeared in connection with a case. Stung by the bug of impatience each demanded to be heard first. This naturally created an unusual situation for the judge. He pondered for a while and then said, "The older of you would be heard first". Neither of them came forward as the very thought of old age was anathema to each.

There is another equally illuminating example which shows the triumph of tact. The French Revolution was in its most intense phase and an excited mob was surging through the streets of Paris. A contingent of soldiers appeared in the streets to disperse the mob. The Commanding Officer was about to order his men to open fire. Just then, a young lieutenant asked permission of the commanding officer to appeal to people. Permission was granted. Riding out in front of the soldiers he doffed his hat and said, "Gentlemen will you have the kindness to retire, for I am ordered to shoot down the rabble". The mob dispersed quietly and thus unnecessary bloodshed was avoided.

Orison Swett Marden has wonderfully put the definition of tact in the following words, "Tact is a combination of good temper, ready wit, quickness of perception and ability to take in the exigency of the occasion instantly. It is never offensive but is a balm, allaying suspicion and soothing".

The secret of all success lies in being alive to what is going on around us; in adjusting oneself to one's surroundings; in being sympathetic and helpful; in knowing the wants of the time; in saying to one's friends and colleagues what they want to hear, what they need to hear at the right moment.

Even the exercise of authority when tempered with tact, produces far greater impact than if it is conditioned with arrogance. Once a group of American soldiers were trying to roll a log of wood to ford a river which was obstructing troop—movement. Despite their best efforts, the soldiers found themselves unable to move the log. The Commanding officer, exasperated by their inability to perform the act, kept shouting orders. He did not pause for a moment to ponder that his lending a helping hand could solve the problem. Intoxicated by the power of his rank he thought it was beneath his dignity to join hands with the soldiers.

Just then, George Washington who was the comander-in-chief happened to pass that way. He took in the situation and went forward to join hands with the soldiers in pushing the log. The work was done within no time. The soldiers thanked him profusely as they had been struggling vainly for hours to accomplish that. While departing George Washington said to the commanding officer, "In future if you fall short of manpower call for Washington." On hearing these words the comanding offficer felt flabbergasted. The message that 'pride is petty' had gone home. Obviously tact achieved much more than admonition which would have left behind a trail of bitterness. Addison says, "A man may not have much learning or wit but if he has common sense and something friendly in his behaviour, it will conciliate men's minds more than the brightest thoughts."

Many accomplish great things with a little ability but more tact. The secret of most businessmen thriving is not their brightly shining talent but the magic power of tact which they have cultivated in abundance. No businessman tries to antagonise his customers. Instead of calling his buyers *customers* he addresses them as his *'patrons.'* The following paragraph in a business letter bears eloquent testimony to how effectively tact is employed by a businessman: "We should be thankful for any information of any dissatisfaction with any former transactions with us and we will take immediate steps to remedy it."

Some people wrongly consider tact as cunning. Hence they shun it. They believe that bluntness is a virtue. In their opinion it shows strength of character. But the truth is otherwise. Calling a blind man blind demonstrates neither one's good manners nor strength of character.

A young man who aspires to go up in life must imbibe the truth that talent at best ensures entry into a profession but it is tact that prevents stagnation and assures a smooth climb. In simple words blend of tact and talent spells success. Try and watch the results. Surely you will get a pleasant surprise.

■■

The Tonic of Courage and Faith

Fear is the arch enemy of courage. It is the acknowledgement, conscious or unconscious of one's own spiritual, moral or physical weakness.

A Roman philosopher Tacitus has said, "The gods look with favour on superior courage". In other words, courage is the hallmark of a builder, an achiever. The history of civilisation is the history of courage which men and women have displayed in different walks of life. "There shall be no Alps," said Napoleon and led his army across the mountains down into Italy and to victory. Lakshmibai, popularly known as "Rani of Jhansi" gave a good account of her unique valour in the battlefield. She was not even 23 when she took the bold decision to spurn the sheltered regal splendour and fight against the British regime to break the shackles of India's slavery. Her martydom will remain an inexhaustible source of inspiration to patriots all over the world. No less inspiring are the patriotic deeds of Bhagat Singh and Chandra Shekhar Azad who sacrificed their Youth at the altar of India's freedom.

Courage in the battlefield is certainly admirable. But no less commendable is its manifestation in other walks of life. Beethoven, an illustrious musician had become stone-deaf at an early age. But the severity of this handicap could not could not subdue his spirit. He produced some of the most memorable melodies after he became deaf. Keats fell a victim to consumptive disease quite early in life. But he did not let the ailment, though fatal it was, to fill him with despondency and paralyse his poetic talent. Some of his detractors subjected him to very scathing criticism and advised him to give up writing poetry and concentrate on his job as a medical assistant which the poet had taken up to earn his living. Keats did not heed such comments and pursued his goal unswervingly. It is a tribute to his indomitable spirit that he succeeded in achieving a permanent niche in the history of English poetry.

In our country the name of Munshi Prem Chand conjures up visions of an unconquerable spirit in the arena of literature. The Munshi had to live in grinding poverty. Gifted as he was with matchless talent, he could readily find other profitable avenues of employment. But he had made a bold resolve to live by the pen and did not deviate from his path even in the face of heavy odds.

The tonic of courage is the finest mental medicine in the world. Courage is born of consciousness of power. It gives serenity and poise to man and sustains him in the most trying circumstances. After vanquishing King Porus, Alexander took him prisoner and asked, "How should I treat you"? "Like a king" replied the unruffled Porus. Obviously defeat had not shattered him. Similarly, when the Greek Government asked Socrates under penalty of death to repudiate his principles, he replied, "I am a citizen, not of Athens or Greece but of the world". Today Socrates is remembered with profound reverence all over the world because he had defended his freedom of thought without fearing death, Confuscius aptly observes, "To know what is right and not to do it is the worst cowardice".

As possession of courage enables a person to occupy a distinguished position in society, lack of it pushes him into ignominious obscurity. What deprives man of his courage? Fear is the arch enemy of courage. "Fear", says Helen Crane, "is the acknowledgement, conscious or unconscious of one's own spiritual, moral or physical weakness. It admits of an inability to cope with a situation; it affirms a powerlessness to act in accordance with one's desires." Indeed, fear keeps man in bondage. It takes a heavy toll of one's energy. It makes one fight a losing battle which he can otherwise win. It will not be an exaggeration to say that fear kills more persons than disease or war. A person who had developed the attitude, "I am afraid I am not going to succeed" is already doomed to failure. A mentally beaten person, even if he has a vast reserve of energy never succeeds in accomplishing his task.

To dispel negative thoughts, you will do well to bear in mind the sage counsel offered by Samuel, "God almighty hates quitters". Do you know who is a quitter? A quitter is one who leaves his work halfdone anticipating failure out of fear for which there is no basis. Shakespeare admonishes such persons thus:

"Cowards die many times before their death,
The valiant never tastes of death but once".

Apart from courage, faith is another important attribute of the human personality that paves one's way to success. Faith is confidence in one's ability to do things, and belief in his friends and colleagues that they would extend whole-hearted cooperation in the project or task he may choose to undertake. Faith or self-confidence influences others tremendously. It spreads like contagion.

Self-confidence is found in ample measure in all great leaders. Gandhi demonstrated wonderful powers of faith while waging a grim fight agaist the British regime to win freedom for India. He wielded more power than any of his contemporaries despite the fact that he had none of the conventional tools of power such as money, battleships, soldiers and other materials of warfare. Dale Carnegie wrote of Gandhi's power of self-confidence thus, "Gandhi has no money, no home, he does not own a suit of clothes, but he does have power. How does he come by that power? He created it out of his understanding of the principle of faith and through his ability to transplant that faith into the minds of two hundred million people".

Another equally illustrious example of faith was of

Winston Churchill. When Hitler declared the Second World War, England was unprepared to face the formidable foe. In fact England reeled under the attack and lay plunged in impenetrable gloom. At that time, not only was Britain's reputation as a great power at stake but its very survival was uncertain. At this critical juncture Britain desperately looked for saviour. Churchill emerged as a shooting star to dispel the gloom of despair from the firmament of England and revived hopes of victory among his compatriots.

How did Curchill proceed to accomplish this uphill task? He had unshakable faith in his ability to lead his people. He also knew that his countrymen were prepared to make any sacrifices to gain victory but they had given way to despondency. In order to stir up once again the sagging spirits of his countrymen, he made a highly inspiring speech which ran thus: "I have nothing to offer to you but blood, toil, tears and sweat. We shall go on to the end, we shall fight on the seas, we shall fight with growing confidence and growing strength in the air. We shall fight in the fields and in the streets. We shall fight in the hills, we shall never surrender."

Obviously courage and faith can wrest success even from the reluctant hands of fate. Courage and faith are by no means the monopoly of a few persons in the world. These twin traits can be cultivated through conscious effort. Shakespeare has said, "Nothing is good or bad but thinking makes it so." In other words, when the mind is changed, the man is changed. Let your mind dwell on brave thoughts and the principle of "Like begets like" will bring about a wonderful improvement in your personality.

■■

Your Decision is Your Destiny

You must not be afraid of making mistakes. Here you will do well to bear in mind that even the wisest person is likely to err.

"Luck decides our place in the world, sometimes," says W.J. Ennever. "You make your own place in the world, almost entirely".

The life story of many a great man proves that. Great men, besides bringing fame and glory to themselves by taking momentous decisions, have vitally influenced the course of world history. Abraham Lincoln's bold decision to end slavery sparked off a fierce revolt against him. But the success of that very decision carved out a place for him in the history of the world. Similarly the great patriots who took bold decisions to sacrifice everything in the cause of the freedom of the country changed the destiny of India by winning freedom for her. Their names are remembered with profound respect in India and are a source of inspiration to freedom fighters in other lands.

The capacity to make bold, prompt and definite decisions plays a very important part in the life of every individual. Leaders in buisiness, industry and other walks of life attain the positions they do because of their power to take important decisions. Anyone who aspires to hold a key position must acquire this power.

Even in our day to day life, the importance of decision making cannot be overlooked. Almost daily we have to take decisions on vital as well as trivial issues. Those who are unable to reach decisions have to suffer.

Procrastination is a common personality defect. Napoleon Hill says, "Procrastination, the opposite of decision-making is a common enemy which practically every man must conquer".

A young man who has not acquired the knack of making sound decisions is never entrusted with important jobs. He is often branded as incompetent by his colleagues and superiors. The habit of indecision, besides rendering his prospects of progress gloomy, also damages his self-respect among the people around him. They poke fun at him for his failing.

The habit of indecision which causes so much agony to man is bred by a number of factors. Sometimes a person may be prevented from taking a decision for fear of failure. At other times lack of proper thinking may induce him to defer decision till it is too late.

To overcome this handicap, first of all one should set a clear cut goal which one wants to achieve. Setting a goal is very important. In the absence of a clear cut goal, decision-making becomes as useless as trying to buy a ticket without determining the destination.

After the goal has been set, one should start collecting the relevant facts and analysing them. This way a clear picture of your intended project will emerge and haziness in thinking will be dispelled. Above all, a thorough knowledge of facts will breed confidence in you.

While you are collecting facts to arrive at a decision, you may seek counsel with some experienced person. There is no harm in that. Indeed it may do some real good to you.

You must not be afraid of making mistakes. Here you will do well to bear in mind that even the wisest person is likely to err. So you should not allow yourself to be unduly obsessed with that fear. After all God has made man in his own image. Let the divinity in you be the best gurantee against mistakes. Moreover, no one can achieve perfection all of a sudden. Before you become an expert rider, you will heave to suffer a good many bruises. As a matter of fact, everyone has to pay the price of attaining perfection, in the form of mistakes. Why should you then hope to be an exception? In fact you should be ready to take occasional lapses in decision-making in your stride and not let them deflate you.

Besides a fear of mistakes, lack of courage also often proves a great hurdle in being able to reach a decision. Here he may seek inspiration from Socrates. Socrates' decision to drink the cup of poison rather than compromise in his personal belief was a decision based on courage. It gave to the people then unborn the right to freedom of thought and speech. Your decision too can be of vital significance in promoting the welfare of others.

The role of the power of decision-making in your personal advancement is quite obvious. This power is rarely a gift of nature. Those who wish to be front-rankers have to make conscious efforts to cultivate it. Others who do not make efforts to acquire it, have to accept the position of back-benchers. The choice whether you would be a frontranker or a back-bencher rests with you.

The Anatomy of Success

Ambition is not something to be afraid or ashamed of. Ambition is a spur to achievement."

A well-dressed person attracts attention immediately in any gathering. Why do you pay attention to him? The secret of his being a cynosure of all eyes is that he has chosen his clothes with special care. Like the well-dressed person a successful person also becomes a centre of attraction. In order to wrap up yourself with the aura of success, you have to pay a price. It is not the others who will make a gift of success to you. Even if it were possible, seeking charity is beneath the dignity of a person who respects his talent, and there is no one who is not endowed with talent. Thus, success is the birthright of every young person. Why should you then incur the stigma of seeking success as alms when you can earn it with dignity through your own efforts. Why should you deliberately make yourself a crippled parasite when God has conferred on you the bounty of energy and intelligence in ample measure?

Milton had become totally blind at 42. Apparently his ambition to write poems should have been blighted. But he did not let even this gerat calamity stand in his way. He dictated his immortal work *Paradise Lost* to his daughters. Like Milton, Hellen too was struck by blindness. But she too did not wallow in her misery. She conquered the darkness through her indomitable spirit and firm determination. She learnt Braille which enabled her to write a number of books that made her a celebrity. Her works won several international awards. When people so afflicted could wrest success from the jaws of formidable odds, persons in favourable circumstances must be able to achieve a larger measure of success. You will certainly agree that this is by no means too high an expectation.

Ambition is not something to be afraid or ashamed of. Your ambition is a spur to achievement. But aspiration is not always achievement. As they say if wishes were horses, beggars would ride. To woo Dame Success, you should grasp the significance of right thinking. When you set out to accomplish a task, your mind is flooded with a large number of ideas. All ideas are not equally important and relevant. You have to learn to eliminate the less important and irrelevant ideas, such weeding out is necessary because irrelevant ideas divert your attention from the main task and retard the pace of your progress. They lead to waste of time and energy. Ideas running riot are as undesirable as a rioting mob.

To entertain and follow up good ideas is only one ingredient of success. They are only the starting point on the road to success. You have to address yourself to the task of translating them into practice in the spirit of do or die. You have to brace yourself so that you do not give up at any stage, never admit defeat, and never quit. Even God hates a quitter, If you do not develop enough grit, you may end up with some idle, unfulfilled day-dreams.

There are some young persons who take up a task with great gusto but let their zeal evaporate when they are midway. Needless to say success always eludes them. Remember, the world applauds only those who reach the peak. The work of quitters is never acclaimed.

Today the people world over revere the names of Tagore, Tenzing, Lincoln and Edward Jenner because they did not give up their chosen goals in disgust when they came face to face with difficulties. On the other hand, they waded through difficulties cheerfully and did not rest until the destination was reached. The significance of pursuit is embodied in the adage: "True genius consists of ten per cent inspiration and ninety per cent perspiration" There is a Chinese proverb: "Great souls have wills, feeble ones have wishes." You are aware that great souls evoke thunderous applause by their unique performance and feeble ones provoke jeers because they invite failure by adopting the line of least resistance.

Surely you do not want to be pushed into obscurity. Sow the seed of success through ambition, nurture and protect it with meticulous care like a sapling against onslaughts of rain and wind. After you have done all that, there is no goal that can elude you.

Ambition—The Spur to Success

By adopting the line of least resistance, we only sow seeds of failure. Success is more enjoyable when it has been won in the face of heavy odds.

What is a ship without a rudder? Can a rudderless ship ever reach its destination? It just drifts and is tossed about by all passing waves and winds. A man without ambition is no better than a rudderless ship. One who has an ambition and works hard to achieve his goal attains glory. No young person worth his salt should be without ambition.

Ambition is very crucial as it provides the first initial impulse that puts one on the road to success. But if the initial impulse is not followed with vigour and determination, nothing can be achieved. You may plant a mango-sapling but thereafter you cannot sit pretty and expect to enjoy delicious fruit. For that you will have to tend, water and protect the plant over a long period of time. It is only after patience and sustained hard work that you will be able to savour its fruit.

All young people wish to make the top grade in life. Some of them begin work with great enthusiasm. But before long many develop cold feet, specially when they come to face difficulties. Difficulties dampen their spirits and wreck their morale. Such persons have only romantic ideas. They are unrealistic and expect roses, roses all the way. When they encounter difficulties in one direction, they change course and so hop from one job to another without making a success of any. Such persons end up as quitters.

A wise person never lets difficulties bar his way to success. He developes grit to conquer them, because he realises that it is sheer folly to abandon effort when success is only a few steps away. By adopting the line of least resistance, we only sow seeds of failure. Success is most enjoyable when it has been won in the face of heavy odds.

Indolence is yet another enemy of ambition. Every young man wants to make good in life but some are allergic to hard work. They flock to a fortune-teller asking for a talisman which may bring them spectacular success without lifting their little finger. Like Mr. Micawber, they live from day to day in the fond hope that something will turn up unexpectedly some day. They little realise that success never favours a sluggard. Someone has rightly said that it is one per cent inspiration and ninety nine per cent perspiration that paves the way to success.

Hard work never kills a man. Indolence does. The will to work is a priceless gift. Some persos become jittery as soon as they set to work. From the outset they are scared of the prospect of failure. Such fears are baseless. Instead one should try to find why one's efforts are not yielding the desired results. The reason may be that the person concerned has become a prisoner of his fears. In a bid to save face, he might say "I am not in a mood today". As a result his work may accumulate and he may ultimately find it difficult to accomplish anything.

You must exert your utmost to cultivate regular habits. Order is heaven's first law. If you are orderly and regular in your working, you can derive as much pleasure from work as from play. Work is worship. Only those who have a worshipful attitude to work make any sort of success.

Take for example Copernicus. He had a burning desire to solve the riddle of the structure of the universe. It was indeed a Herculean task. Till that time scientists had been following the Ptolemic theory which considered the earth as the centre of the universe.

Copernicus lay at night observing the movements of stars and other planets and expounded a theory placing the sun at the centre of the universe, with the earth and other planets revolving round it. This provoked the wrath of clergymen who considered the Ptolemic theory as sacrosanct. But Copernicus had blazed a new trail which could not be obliterated by ecclesiastical bigotry. He stuck to his guns. By adopting a bold, non-conformist approach, he encouraged further research. His work formed the foundation upon which Galileo, Newton, Einstein and others laid the foundation of modern astronomy.

That goes to show that if you are sincerely in love with your ambition, success cannot elude you. But if you are flirting with it, failure is certain. Those who fall a prey to complacency lose sight of their goal and are condemned to a humdrum existence. They have not learnt, "To strive, to seek, to find and not to yield."

Be sure you do not belong to that category. You have two valuable assets—youth and talent. And these are the best planks of your success. Some say that they are underprivileged and have no one in influential circles to push them up the ladder of success. True, there are people in this country who make the top grade through nepotism. But is seeking charity a graceful thing? Should a normal human being with healthy legs seek the aid of crutches to walk to his destination?

History is full of examples of persons who were underprivileged but made their way to the top through relentless hard work. Abraham Lincoln did not have even a rusty dime to finance his education. He lived in the obscurity of a dingy long cabin. Who could imagine that such a lad would one day be the President of the U.S.A. and be included among the all-time greats of history? So being underprivileged should be no excuse to deprive you of success. If you want to count for something in life, brush aside alibis for inaction and start right now from where you are. Whenever doubts assail your mind remember the Chinese proverb which says, "Great souls have wills, feeble ones have only wishes". ■■

Don't Be a Grievance Collector

Good manners are the essential characteristic of a successful person. One should not abandon decency even while the going is rough!

Last month a college in our town arranged a debate. My neighbour Prem was one of the participants in the debate. He is preparing for the B.A. final examination this year. Intelligent and hardworking, he has a desire to excel in studies and other extracurricular activities. He was all earnest about the debate. He read several books and magazines to fish out new material concerning the topic, sought guidance from his teachers, and above all rehearsed a lot before finally participating in the debate. As Prem went to take part in the debate he was in cheerful mood, a reflection of confidence which his preparation had bred in him.

In the evening when I met Prem I enquired of his performance in the debate. He replied morosely, "I have been awarded only third prize," He added, "I am certain that the judges were prejudiced, partial." He tried to prove his contention by pouring plain abuse on the judges for their alleged favouritism.

There is nothing wrong for a young student to aspire for the highest recognition. But this need not make him obvious of the fact that other young persons too are talented. Their performance can be equally good, sometimes better even. A young man who conjures up the wrong image of himself and thinks that he alone is the embodiment of excellence is in for disillusionment.

To avoid crippling frustration a young man should develop balanced outlook on life. For instance, Prem instead of feeling broken-hearted and nourishing a grievance against the judges for their verdict should have enjoyed the measure of success he had achieved. After all his not getting the first prize did not mean the dead end of the road to success. Thus Prem instead of wallowing in the sorrow should have utilized the occasion to evaluate his performance objectively and found out what had gone wrong. Such an approach paves way for greater success in future as objective reappraisal enables a person to eschew mistakes.

Kailash had the ambition to scale peaks in the business world. Considering Kailash's resources and dash, achievement of his goal did not appear impossible. He set up a shop in a posh locality. Now everyone thought that the achievement of his goal was only a matter of time. But after two years he found himself nowhere nearer his goal. Why did success elude him? Were there not many customers to patronise his shop that he did not earn enough profits? For sometime he had a bumper sale. But then suddenly inflation set in which made prices soar higher and higher. Customers became price-conscious and began to display much disinclination in buying things. Kailash did not like this behaviour of his customers. If any customer after seeing a thing did not buy it he lost the temper with him. His irritable temperament struck a blow to his business by scaring away his customers. Some offended customers told him bluntly, "We do not buy anything from you for nothing. When we have to pay a price why should we not examine the quality of a thing?"

Decency Pays

Now Kailash grumbles that people have withdrawn their patronage. He should know that no one can expect a cow to yield milk after it has been beaten. Likewise no amount of grumbling can enable a businessman to boost his sales if he has scared them away by his insolent behaviour. Good manners are the essential characteristics of a successful businessman. He does not abandon decency even while the going is rough. He is fully aware that patience displayed in handling customers during a lean period does not go in vain. Indeed it preserves their goodwill which brings rich rewards when the situation takes a favourable turn.

Madan has an ambition to see his name in print in magazines and newspapers. To realise his ambition sometime back he wrote four articles for different magazines and after despatching them eagerly waited for their acceptance. Unluckily after a few days he received back all his articles with rejection slips. This aroused a sharp reaction in him. He accused the editors of showing prejudice against him by not accepting his articles. To defend his failure he said, "Editors dole out patronage to their minions only."

Evidently Madan discounts hard work as a means to success and believes that flattery is the only passport to success. If Madan instead of wasting his time and energy in nursing a grievance against editors sets on the task of reviewing his articles to remove the possible defects he can certainly improve his chances of winning an editorial favour.

As long as Madan does not realize that real success is never offered to anyone on a silver platter, success will continue to evade him like a mirage. To bask in the glory of real success one has to slog a lot and prove his worth.

A teacher who wishes to get proper response from his students must dish out fresh stimulating academic material. This approach can make the classroom as active a place for students as the movie hall. For this the teacher has to take enough pains to equip himself with new material by regularly studying books, magazines and standard works. To win respect from students a teacher must show love and respect to his pupils. For this he must give up the old notion that youngsters are like a herd to be driven with a stick. They are human beings and should be treated as such. The teacher should not be content with teaching the proverb

"Love begets love" for examination purpose only but also practise it himself while dealing with his students. Harold Sherman rightly says, "What you are not, you can never be, until and unless you do something about it."

There are some who do have grievances not only against their neighbours, colleagues, customers and students but also against fate. They think that if fate had not conspired against them they would have attained peaks of success. But history is replete with cases of people who rose to eminence undeterred by their adverse circumstances. V.S. Srinivasa Sastri was born in a poor family yet he became a great man of our time. He started his career as a humble school teacher and finally transformed himself into a matchless orator, academician and leader through sheer hard work.

Nothing but Friends

Lincoln was so poor that when he was elected to the legislature of his State he borrowed money to buy a set of clothes so that he might make a respectable appearance. Again when he was elected President of America he borrowed money from a friend to move his family to Washington. Evidently he did not allow poverty to block his way to success. What was the secret of his success? When qualifications of different Presidential candidates were being discussed and Lincoln's name was mentioned, someone said, "Lincoln has nothing, only plenty of friends." This shows that one of the planks of Lincoln's success was his tremendous magnanimity. A magnanimous man hardly gets an occasion to have a grouse against others. Even if someone hurts him deliberately he readily forgives the lapse and forgets the unpleasant experience. He knows that people are not normally unkind or unjust. The snub or neglect he was suffered may be due to another person's inadvertence or preoccupation.

Next time before you pick up a grievance against someone, ask yourself, "What have you done for others that you should expect such tender consideration from them?" This approach will prevent the grievance from sinking solved into your subconscious to breed like poisonous bacteria in your emotional blood stream.

Even if you have a genuine grievance it is not worthwhile to put it in a glass case and gloat over it. Katherine Mansfield says, "Make a rule of life never to regret and never look back. Regret is an appalling waste of energy. You cannot build on it." Indeed life is what we make it. Why should we then not build life on generosity and optimism which are antidotes to grievance-collecting?

Rewards of Right Thinking

It is futile to blame luck or circumstances for the failure which one deliberately invites through lethargy. It is not at all impossible to enjoy a certain measure of prosperity if one is willing to put necessary effort in the right direction.

Naresh is intelligent, young and ambitious. He also has adequate monetary resources. Obviously he has all the ingredients of success, yet he has been trying in vain to achieve success. Sometime back he set up a conduit factory considering it to be a profitable venture. He expected instant success in the project; he dreamt that within a short period he would earn fabulous profits and live elegantly. For sometime the products of his factory were in large demand which enabled him to reap good dividends. His initial success indicated that very soon his ambition would fructify.

But soon his business came to be rocked by price fluctuations in the market. Naresh found this situation highly unpalatable. Instead of coping with it by displaying grit and patience he succumbed to despair. He began to rue the day he had made the decision to go into business. So desperate was he that he sold his factory at a heavy loss. The man who bought Naresh's factory was optimistic that the uneasy situation would not continue for ever. His conviction came true and soon he became prosperous.

Having sold the factory Naresh joined a bank to have a steady income. But his salary was far from adequate for providing him the luxuries he had been dreaming about. Now Naresh, instead of preparing for a departmental exam to improve his professional and economic status, let himself be constantly distracted by the craving to enjoy luxuries. This obsession paralysed his power of thinking and destroyed his peace of mind. One day he chose to resign his job in the bank in utter disgust.

Following his ill-conceived step to resign, Naresh would have found himself in a miserable plight, if his father had not come to his rescue. His father used his personal influence to get him a job in a rapidly growing firm. Naresh was happy for sometime as the job was both well-paid and prestigious. After four years he felt disillusioned and embittered when his junior Rajinder was chosen for promotion ignoring him.

Why was Naresh denied the opportunity to climb up the professional ladder? Naresh always shirked the responsibities entrusted to him by his superiors, while Rajinder always did a little more than he was asked to do. He believed that talent was futile without matching efforts. Clearly he was guided by the motto: no sweetness without sweat. No doubt Naresh too was equally talented but he was reluctant to maximise the use of his intellectual powers and relied on his father's influence to push him up.

It is futile to blame luck or circumstances for the failure which one deliberately invites through lethargy. It is not at all impossible to enjoy a certain measure of prosperity if one is willing to put necessary effort in the right direction.

A Mouthful of Hay

Prosperity begins in the mind and its attainment is impossible when the mental attitude is hostile to it. There is no philosophy which will help a man to succeed when he is always doubting his ability or blaming his circumstances. There is an adage: "Every time the sheep bleats it loses a mouthful of hay." Similarly you lose your energy and cripple your talent every time you allow yourself to complain of your lot saying; "I can never do what others do. I am a failure because luck is against me."

Right thinking means positive attitude toward work. A fatal penalty awaits those who look upon work as punishment and not an opportunity to display their ability. I know Sunil who some years ago started a general store on the modest scale as he had a limited capital at his disposal. His greatest asset was that he had set his heart on achieving success and resolved not to be discouraged by setbacks. The success did not come to him readily, rather he had to achieve success the hard way. Quite often his sales were very modest as other stores in his neighbourhood being better stocked could attract his customers by offering them a wide variety. Sometimes he could not replenish his stocks for lack of money. But he contended against all these odds with courage and equanimity and took them in his stride. Eventually he succeeded in transforming his small store into a big departmental store.

The secret of his success apart from his courage and patience to face difficulties was his pragmatism in economic matters. Sunil displayed vision in managing his financial affairs. He ploughed back a major share of his profits into business rather than squander them on personal comforts. He was fully aware that personal comforts could wait till he stood on a firm footing in his business. He was guided by the philosophy that in the initial stage money is much more worth if invested to keep the shop better stocked with goods rather than spend it in acquiring status symbols like modern gadgets or in keeping an enviable wardrobe.

True long-term planning is necessary to ensure essential success of any venture but at the same time it should be borne in mind that if one has an unusually long spell of fruitless efforts he is likely to fall a prey to despodency. Such a situation can be warded off by providing short-term goals which should sustain one's interests enabling oneself to taste success at regular intervals.

Right thinking is needed as much to ensure probable success as to preserve domestic harmony. Shekhar has allowed his wife to take up job so that their combined income might enable them to lead a clean and comfortable life. Economically they are well off now. But in their relations, an under-current tension has developed of late which erupts at times.

Not that Shekhar's wife has become less devoted and less loyal after she has taken up the job. Her job and housekeeping do not leave much time for her to look after the needs of her husband the way she did before. But Shekhar does not take into account the changed situation. He expects her to pay the same personal attention to him as she did earlier. As such their mutual relations are marred by unseemly conflicts. Shekhar's wife feels baffled and does not know how to avoid bitterness in her marital relations. She suggests to her husband quite often that she would give up her job to become a whole time housewife which will enable her to pay more personal attention to him. But Shekhar is not willing to accept this proposal as this involves financial squeeze. His wife thus continues to be tormented by his inconsiderate attitude.

Shekhar will do well to bear in mind that one can't have his cake and eat it too. He should realize that his wife too is a human being. Apart from job she has to bear the strain of housekeeping. Naturally she feels tired having to do all the chores throughout the day. In such circumstances Shekhar must take into account his wife's difficulties before accusing her of being indiffierent to him. He should also learn to sacrifice his personal comforts a little in order to enjoy the economic benefits of his wife's work. Rationalism rather than narcissism helps a lot in such matters. Right thinking is undoubtedly an open sesame to professional success and domestic harmony.

How to Enjoy Your Work

True enjoyment from work does not come if constantly obsessed with monetary rewards. Money is certainly needed to keep body and soul together. But nourishment of skill is much more important than keeping yourself alive.

'The man who will not work,' says St Paul, 'must be left to starve.' In other words, indolence is a curse which must be eschewed at all costs. Through optimum use of his inherent powers man does not only wrap up himself with glory of success but also wins gratitude of his fellow-beings by contributing to their happiness.

True enjoyment from work does not come if one is constantly obsessed with monetary rewards. There is a craftsman in our city who is endowed with a unique skill for embroidering sarees. He has always much more work than he can cope with. He has been following a golden principle since he started his work several years ago. He accepts only that much work which he can finish to his own entire satisfaction within the period appointed with his customers. As a result many female customers of his go away disappointed, particularly those who want to get their work done urgently. If this craftsman lowers the quality of his work a little, he can do much more work and thereby push up his earnings considerably. But he does not succumb to this temptation.

One day when I visited his shop I made this suggestion to him. On hearing my words his conscience was deeply pricked and he replied, "Sir, money is certainly needed to keep body and soul together. But nourishment of skill is much more important than keeping yourself alive. Man dies and skill survives.' To drive home further the truth of his point he told me the names of several illustrious painters, sculptors and musicians who showed singular dedication to their art not motivated exclusively by monetary considerations and thus lent eternal glory to their skills and made them a source of perennial inspiration to future generations of artists and craftsmen.

I was profoundly impressed by this semi-literate craftsman's vision and zeal for his work. His words contained a million dollar truth that cultivation of a skill for exclusively pecuniary purposes destroys its creative excellence. Indeed every talented person who is genuinely in love with skill considers it an affront to use it for purely monetary gains.

Charles F Kettering rightly observes: 'If we look through history, we can't help but be impressed by the fact that some of the most important inventions were made by men who were not primarily seeking financial gains but rather were working for something just because they wanted to do it.'

He goes on, 'The names of these men are legion; Edison, Goodyear, Wright brothers and Graham Bell are just a few pioneers who possessed this driving urge. And those who have experienced the thrill of a successful experiment know the satisfaction of accomplishment that far surpasses the monetary reward which may or may not be coming.'

A man who loves his work sincerely also possesses tremendous patience. He is never satisfied with the slipshod product. Even if he has to re-do it dozen times to improve its quality, he never minds it and is never filled with disgust. There is a classic example of Balzac, the French novelist, who started one of his novels seventeen times. Such people are indeed crazy about the quality of their work. This is why they leave behind immortal traditions for others to follow.

True, a job well-done brings immense delight to the doer. But the skill to perform a job excellently can't be acquired in a single attempt. For this a lot of vision, patience and meticulous planning are needed. If this fact is disregarded, the net result is disaster and frustration. Ramesh's friend Sajan is ambitious and has a lot of zeal for work. Three years ago Sajan set up a ginning factory which is now a highly profitable preposition. Encouraged by Sajan's success Ramesh too set up a ginning factory at another place. He invested a sizable capital to ensure success of his venture. But as soon as he began to encounter difficulties all his enthusiasm vanished just as does mist after the sunrise. Consequently he suffered a crushing loss.

All this disaster occurred because Ramesh did not understand the real means or zest for work. Zest for work is not temporary phenomenon like a flash of lightning. Exuberant attitude towards work to be transformed into a perpetual rather than a momentary flash of lightning case you wish to enjoy the glory of success. Baudelaire used to say, 'I grew up on leisum. He did not mean that he loved indolence. In fact it implies deeper reflection and careful planning.

Like Ramesh, Usha too has a wrong notion about zeal for work. She is young and ebullient. She works as a private secretary in a business firm. When her boss asks her to type out business letters, she finishes them within a few minutes. But when she places them before her boss he finds them full of typing errors. This brings Usha admonition rather than appreciation. Snubs apart she has to redo that work again. All those who work in slapdash manner, the thrill of joy that emerged from a job well-accomplished always comes to evade them. Above all by their lackadaisical working habits they fall in the estimation of their superiors and thus render their chances of promotion bleak.

Bear in mind that speed at the cost of efficiency is never a manifestation of enthusiasm for work.

There is a shining example of Dr Meghnad Saha who because of his unstinted devotion to work attained pinnacle of scientific glory even under the British Government in India when the native talent was generally poorly rated. Dr Saha being the son of poor parents could pursue his studies only because of generous scholarships given to him by his father's friends. Saha's passionate pursuit of science finally blossomed into 'Thermal Ionization Theory' which appeared in the Philosophical Magazine of London in 1920 and brought him a unique fame. Saha's idea brought in new thinking in astrophysics which helped scientists understand the colour and compositions of stars, a field where no scientific explanation had existed before. The exciting adventure of Dr. Saha's demonstrates how a man of determination and zeal can transform his destiny by turning obstacles into incentives.

> A positive work-attitude, is as good as money in the bank. Anyone who does not assimilate this truth and manifest it in his daily endeavours is sure to be pushed into the limbo of failure and ablivion. Instead of enjoying the bliss of success and happiness, he has to live with tormenting frustration as a constant bed-feloow.

It is not necessary that enjoyment stems from the pursuit of a unique work alone. Positive work-attitude can even make a daily routine a highly delightful affair which many consider a dreary drudgery. Miss Pushpa works as a salesgirl in a departmental store. While dealing with her customers she displays tremendous patience, charm and tact. She says that many times she has to deal with such customers whose whimsical choice regarding certain articles becomes extremely difficult to satisfy. After seeing dozens of articles they reject them all for one reason or the other and walk away without shopping anything.

In such circumstances, she syas, she was to exercise a good deal of self-control to be pleasant with them as fretting and fuming can spell disaster because the offended customer would never visit the shop again. Besides, he will tell many others not to do shopping at their store. All this will adversely affect the image of their shop and put their business at stake with which her living is vitally linked.

Her employer is fully aware of her affable nature and wonderful tactfulness she displays in boosting sales. Already she has received pay hikes several times. Now she is tipped for promotion to be a sales-supervisor very shortly. Apart from pecuniary rewards she has gained special respect in the eyes of her boss which must be pretty soothing to her heart.

Commenting on how to enjoy your work J Edgar Hoover says, 'The enjoyment depends upon the manner in which the individual accepts its challenge. When a man embarks on a task with a high heart and the will to win, he is almost certain to enjoy his endeavours. But if he attacks his task half-heartedly, fearfully and shackled by self-doubts, his labour becomes an intolerable burden.'

A positive work-attitude is as good as money in the bank. Anyone who does not assimilate this truth and manifest it in his daily endeavours is sure to be pushed into the limbo of failure and oblivion. Instead of enjoying the bliss to success and happiness he has to live with tormenting frustration as a constant bed-fellow.

Rewards of Creative Living

A person with strong will makes earnest efforts to achieve his cherished goal. He is willing to pay any price to enjoy the aura of success.

According to work ethic people may be divided into two categories: those who are willing to work and those who are made to work. Those who are willing to work need no external motivation. They are self-propelled people. They set their own work schedule and go about the job according to the pace determined by them. Those who are made to work belong to the category of reluctant doers. Such persons usually turn out shoddy work. No wonder their performance brings them admonition rather than admiration.

Needless to say it is the positive work ethic that places a person on the pinnacle of glory and the negative work ethic pushes him into the pit where gloom prevails. Work ethic is beautifully embodied in an ancient Chinese proverb which says, "Great souls have wills, feeble ones have only wishes." A person with a strong will makes earnest efforts to achieve his cherished goal. He is undaunted by difficulties. He is willing to pay any price to enjoy the aura of success. On the other hand one who has only a wish is an idle dreamer. He is not a doer. No wonder his utopian schemes bring him jeers rather than cheers from people around him.

It is rightly said that we do not get what we desire; we get what we deserve. We all are endowed with some talent or the other. No human being is devoid of talent. Why do then some succeed and others fail? The reason is not far to seek. Successful people make earnest efforts to nurture their talent. Their motto is: slogging is success. They vigorously pursue their goal until it is achieved.

Those who fail make no efforts to nurture their talent. They are utopian thinkers. They always wait for a miracle or a windfall to happen. In other words, they let complacency blight their talents. Needless to say despair is the inevitable lot of such persons. Instead of basking in the glory of success they are condemned to lead a life of drudgery.

Lives of great men and women bear testimony to the fact that fortune favours the prepared mind. Those who work sincerely win in the long run. Obviously they do not expect success to be offered to them on a silver platter without deserving it first.

Marie Curie's name needs no introduction as it will continue to shine eternally in the firmament of science. In 1891 when Marie from Poland came to the famous university of Sorbonne in Paris gender prejudice was deeprooted even in European countries and girls were considered unfit to study science. When one of her professors saw her in the class he commented, "I see we have a young lady in the class. What is she doing here instead of spending her time in the kitchen"? But Marie did not let such barbed comments dampen her zeal and by her outstanding performance won her teachers' hearts. Behind Marie's immortal scientific achievements lay years of slogging. Her diary informs us, "In a miserable old shed, we spent the best and happiest years of our lives, entirely consecrated to our scientific work, Sometimes, I spent a whole day stirring a boiling mass of pitch blende, with an iron rod nearly as big as my self. By evening my back was broken with fatigue."

For thirty five years Marie Curie handled radium without the protection, later provided to researchers using harmful substances. This exposure caused her body irreparable damage. But she considered it too trivial a price for the benefit the world had gained through the risks she had taken.

Leave normal humans alone the handicapped too have not let their disabilities stand in the path of their progress. Instead of ruing over their afflictions they set out to find ways to overcome them. Every lover of western music knows about Beethoven's soul-stirring symphonies. A noted music critic Ernest Newman says, "It is the peculiarity of Beethoven's imagination that again and again he lifts us to height from which we revaluate not only music but all life, all emotion and all thought."

Beethoven's climb to this dizzy success was not a cake walk. Deafness came to afflict him while he was young. Obviously this ailment threatened to shatter all his dreams of becoming a great musician and he felt perturbed and tormented for some time. Following lines describe his mental torment born of his deafness. Beethoven told his friends and well-wishers, "It is impossible for me to live in the city. Shout for I am deaf. It is humiliation I shall not endure. Let me suffer my silence in solitude."

Apparently remorseless tragedy seemed to trample him to dust. But fortunately this was not to be. As Beethoven was determined to succeed in his chosen vocation at any cost his deafness proved as spur rather than a scourge. Success is indeed most enjoyable when it is won against heavy odds. Beethoven's is by no means an isolated example. This list is indeed interminable. Surdas, a noted Hindi poet and John Milton an immortal English poet and playwright both were victims of blindness. But they did not let their handicap have a last laugh. Through sheer determination and perseverance they created a niche for themselves in the galaxy of creative writers. We all know that the charm of their accomplishments will never wither away and continue to inspire future generations of readers.

Indeed no young person worth his salt seeks success as charity. His motto is: First deserve then desire. To show his worth he accepts challenges and does not let despair cripple his efforts. Those who really deserve Dame, Success always smiles on them. History attests this fact. ■■

Learn The Magic Power of Words

Words are indeed life-blood of human communication. Words that flowed from the mouth of great personages like Gandhi, Confucius and Lincoln have become immortal utterances and are perennial sources of inspiration of mankind.

Desire for communication is inherent in every human being. Even an infant tries to communicate his feelings and needs through sounds and cries which often seem incoherent and incomprehensible. ·But to mother every gesture and sound of the infant is quite intelligible.

As a matter of fact the child picks up rudiments of language skill while he is in the lap of his mother. For this very reason language is popularly called mother-tongue. It is worth while to dispel the wide spread notion that the pre-school child is wholly devoid of language skill. The pre-school child does have a language skill which is yet in a crude form. The school seeks to refine and enrich it by making the child concentrate on vocabulary which will build his future links with religion, society, business, industry and profession.

As a young adult he becomes fully aware of the significance of language skill in his interaction with his family, friends, customers and colleagues. In other words, his success in this spectrum of relationship is determined by how effectively he is able to communicate with others at home, at his work place and in his social circle. If a person is proficient in communication skill he promptly demolishes the barrier of hostility and turns foes into friends. People listen to him with rapt attention. Such a person gets creative cooperation from others. People around him are always eager to place their service at his disposal. His words carry weight with everyone. He is not considered a spoil sport in any social group. On the other hand his company is much sought after by everyone because his words reveal his trust, worthiness and excellence of judgment.

Truly speaking words are powerful tools in our hands. They rule our lives and create consequences. Every husband knows that a few words of endearment quickly soothe the frayed tempers of his work-weary wife. Indeed everyone has a desire to be recognized and praised for a job well-done by him. A person who has to supervise others' work is aware of the fact that praise and encouragement create good end results and hence he is never miserly in doling out words of praise.

Powerful impact of words is not confined to family, work place and social circle. Indeed words have a cataclysmic effect. Virile words can rock the world with force of dynamite. They create tremendous intellectual ferment. Their force transcends electricity, even atomic energy.

Words that flowed from the mouths of great personages like Socrates, Gandhi, Confucius and Lincoln have become immortal utterances and are perennial sources of inspiration for mankind. Just three words "equality, liberty, fraternity" that constituted the slogan of the famous "French Revolution" powerfully influenced political thinking worldwide and heralded a great revolution in global polity whose impact is felt even today. Abraham Lincoln's famous utterance "America can't remain half slave and half free" gave a mortal flow to slavery and thereby radically changed the concept of human values. In India Tilak's inspiring slogan "Freedom is my birth right" had given a tremendous boost to the liberation struggle in the country.

Prof. Kelly Jamison underlines the significance of communication skill thus, "The moment you develop this awareness of words your personal drive begins." Confucius, the famous sage of China, explaining the connotation of the word virtue says, "Five things constitute virtue. They are courtesy, magnanimity, sincerity, earnestness and kindness, With courtesy you avoid insult. With magnanimity you win all. With sincerity men will come to trust you. With earnestness and kindness you can achieve success."

Words are indeed life-blood of human communication. By erroneously using the adage "Silence is golden" you take away words and see what happens. You are virtually dead. You exist as a vegetable. As long as you use words even if you abuse them as politicians often do, you are animate. Animation and articulation are inseparable.

People in all professions education, business, industry, law and mass media have to learn to use words to their advantage. They are aware of the fact that greatest power at man's disposal are words. By making a judicious selection of words in their speech and correspondence people enhance the appeal of their personality.

Words are pregnant with meaning. Through words you can conquer people's hearts because genesis of change lies in them. Through words we give others the feeling of trust worthiness. No wonder we win over people through suggestions and not imposition. Coercion repels people and persuasion attracts them. This is the secret of effective communication.

Needless to stress the fact that communication is a most important skill in life. It provides us an excellent opportunity to explore our capabilities and know the impact of their message on others. So if you wish to perform at peak level, prepare an action plan to develop this skill as its acquisition will open vistas of a sparkling new world for you. Alternative to this in the modern competitive world is to be content with mediocrity and obscurity - a state without name and fame.

Need to Spread Moral Sunshine

"Sophistication in behaviour is the first step that leads man to strangulate morality. It knocks out sincerity which is the basis of morality"

A Hunt, a writer poetically explains the significance of morality thus:

"It is the stainless soul within,
That outshines the fairest skin."

Purity in thinking is a distinctive badge of a noble person. A man will be what his most cherished feelings are. If the heart is not pure, thoughts can't be pure. Purity is revealed by transparency of character. No other treasure in this world is as rich as the consciousness of purity. Contagion of corruption begins to pervert our mind when we start harbouring evil thoughts. In other words, genesis of moral degradation dwells in our thinking.

Sophistication in behaviour is the first step that leads man to strangulate morality. To display sophisticated behaviour man pretends to be what he is not. Thus sophistication knocks out sincerity which is the basis of morality. A sophisticated man becomes a mask-wearer and all his efforts are devoted to concealing what his wrong doings are loudly proclaiming. In this way his life becomes sago of gimmicks.

However skilfully a man may commit misdeeds and throw dust in the eyes of law, their consciousness begins to prick him provided he has not become a hardened criminal. This pricking of conscience gradually becomes unbearable. To get out of this situation he sometimes resorts to a few acts of social welfare and also undertakes to organise religious congregations.

Prayer in itself is a highly ennobling thing. It acts as a detergent to purge us of the dirt of our evil deeds committed unknowingly and sometimes knowingly. But a prayer becomes a sort of gimmick when a person deliberately indulges in evil activities day in and day out and yet offers prayers in the fond hope of being redeemed. We all know that proper use of drug cures one off ailment and its abuse is pernicious. Interestingly a pseudo-spiritualist is no different from a drug-addict. Both are victims of self-deception. To a pseudo-spiritualist salvation is a mirage. To a drug-addict bliss of sound health is elusive.

As a matter of fact morality is the cry of all and the game of the few. Most people wish to have the best of both the worlds-enjoyment of worldly comforts and enjoyment of spiritual glory. Man's desire to eat the cake and have it too, has been responsible for spawning the current spate of scams. Obviously modern man instead of enlightening himself is harnessing education to devise newer and newer techniques of debasement. This is evident from the fact that all scamsters have had the benefit of university education.

Economic offences committed by them unlike the petty economic offences of the illiterate and literate, are a matter of grave concern as they can throw national economy out of gear. Driven by the concern the government has made several attempts from time to time to contain this cancer of corruption but to no avail.

The reason is not far to seek. The fault lies not in our legislation but in ourselves that we are underlings. There is no need to find fault with existing laws as they are quite good to take care of economic offences. It is the man who operates them that needs mending. The man who wields power has no scruples in bending laws to feather his own nest. He dons spiritual robes in public but perpetrates the most reprehensible acts furtively. His dubious behaviour transforms him into a devil quoting scripture. If man really wishes to live up to the adage that God has created him in his own image, then instead of attempting to reforn others by hollow preaching he should sincerely follow the dictim: Doctors cure thyself first.

■■

Is Your Marital Boat Sailing Smoothly?

Although the sex drive is the force that brings two persons together, it is not necessarily the force that keeps them together."

Shyam was married just two years ago. At the time of his marriage he felt that he was destined to enjoy interminable marital bliss. His wife Kalpana was educated and had charming manners. But his fascination for her soon began to fade fast. He nostalgically recalls the days when he was a bachelor. He curses the day he was married and often tells his friends, "I have committed a blunder by marrying. I should have remained single."

Why does marital happiness evade Shyam? Has his wife abandoned sweet manners after marriage and turned a shrewd? Kalpana has not at all said good-bye to her sweet manners. In fact Shyam is to blame himself for the unpleasant situation in which he finds. Before marriage Shyam had to look after himself alone. His salary was spent on seeing movies and visiting fashionable restaurants in the city. After marriage the situation altered. Now in addition to his personal needs he is required to cater to the needs of his wife also. Shyam does not recognise this fact. He persists in his old extravagant habits. If his wife asks him for money to buy groceries and other requirements he tells her, "Try to manage somehow." Kalpana explains to him that it is not possible to buy things on credit as the grocer's bill for the past two months remains unpaid.

At this Shyam peevishly tells Kalpana, "Go to your father and get some money from him." She refuses to do so as she is fully aware that her father has his own family to support. She angrily demands, "Shyam, you must exercise self-restraint in spending. We can't be life-long parasites on others, particularly when you are earning." She adds, "You should know that after a few years, apart from our personal expenses we shall have to bear expenses of our son's education. For all this, we need money."

Shyam dismisses it as a curtain lecture and thinks that "Silence is golden" is the best solution. If Shyam thinks that by turning a deaf ear to what Kalpana says he will be able to enjoy happiness, he is only nourishing an illusion. Shyam should know that by facing the situation squarely alone, he can expect to enjoy conjugal life. Marriage brings certain responsibilities in its wake. Before marriage one has to provide for oneself and after marriage one has to provide for one's spouse and children also. So a married man must curtail his spending to save enough to provide a reasonably decent and comfortable life to his family. Narcissism on the part of husband spells disaster in marriage. Marital bliss is like the perfume of a flower which you can't enjoy without taking proper care of the family plant.

Manohar's case is different from that of Shyam. Manohar has a well-paid job. He also saves enough to fulfil the needs of his family. He has polite and sophisticated demeanour which has made him immensely popular with his colleagues. While dealing with his female colleagues he is even extra nice. But at home he behaves quite differently. At the slightest provocation he gives a mouthful of nasty abuses to his wife and even thrashes her. He does not hesitate to display this savage behaviour towards his wife even before outsiders. As long as he stays at home his wife is awfully tense. Worse still, her children have ceased to respect her and defy her openly.

Manohar's ruthless behaviour has completely shattered his wife's self-confidence as a result of which she is always in a sullen mood. He often feels jealous of his friends when he learns from them that their wives show tremendous love towards them. Manohar should bear in mind that a flower may give perfume even if it is crushed, but it is different with a wife. To enjoy your wife's love you must make yourself worthy of it by treating her with love. Your wife needs to be treated with the same courtesy and affection, even more, as you do the women outside your home. Affection of the husband touches the innermost chords of the wife's heart and she pours forth her purest love for him to feast on.

Neelam says, "My husband makes me feel insignificant like a dumb animal while we visit our friends. He ridicules me and plays up every fault of mine. I feel like running away like a wounded creature. I keep my mouth shut for fear of severe retaliation." Neelam's husband will do well to remember that true love is never born of fear. Nor does derision beget love. You yourself would not shower love and respect on a person who hurls jibes at you. How do you then expect your wife to kiss you while you deliberately kick her? Words may not break bones but they cause wounds which are difficult to heal. It is rightly said: "If one is honoured the other is exalted; if one is dishonoured the other is debased."

Mrs. Bhatia has a grouse against her husband because he is too much demanding in matters of sex. He frequently makes her submit to sex act much against her desire. Not only this, he even demands sex before his own grown up children. When his wife tells him that such a thing will have a pernicious effect on the sensitive minds of their children, he uses foul language and tries to silence her by saying that they will also do the same thing after sometime. What a perverse logic! One wonders if marriage gives a licence for bestiality. Is it really desirable that men indulge in gratification of their sex urge openly as animals copulate by the roadside? As a matter of fact sex act yields true pleasure only when it is done in the privacy of your bedroom and with the consent of your spouse.

Dr. Daniel says, "Although the sex drive is the force that brings two persons together, it is not necessarily the force that keeps them together."

Ranjit is a top executive in a big industrial firm. In his day to day life he has to deal with a number of knotty problems. Sometimes some problems defy solutions and thus leave his mind tense. He returns home in this ruffled state of mind, takes his meals hurriedly in a perfunctory manner and retires to bed without talking to his wife or children. When his wife finds him in a sullen mood she coaxes him to open his heart but he persists in keeping silent. Ranjit thinks that his wife is not competent enough to untie the knots of the problems facing him and thus it is futile to discuss them with her.

True, his wife does not possess the professional expertise but sometimes commonsense too works miracles. Moreover, the wife enables her husband to tide over an unpleasant situation by whispering into his ears words of encouragement which no one else can do. Also sharing her husband's burden gratifies the wife's ego much.

A man who sincerely wishes to enjoy pleasures of a happy home life should heed the advice of Patience Strong. He says, "Love is something more than kisses on a wedding day, it is facing life together, all the while and all the way."

■■

Way to Cultural Excellence

Good persons move about fearlessly at all hours. There is no need for them to make their activities clandestine.

It goes without saying that light and darkness have always existed in the world. Man avoids darkness and seeks light. The reason is not far to seek. Darkness fills him with fear and light generates in him hope and confidence. In other words darkness is a symbol of evil deeds and light is associated with virtuous deeds. All bad characters operate under the cover of darkness. Their movements by and large are restricted during broad day light. On the contrary good persons move about fearlessly at all hours. There is no need for them to make their activities clandestine.

What prompts a man to engage himself in any activity good or bad? Desire is the first thing that prompts him to action. Man then evaluates the result of his action. Passing judgement he says. "This being good ought to be done. That being bad, ought not to be done". All these evaluations are not equally valid. The reason is that we usually pass judgement on the basis of our likes and dislikes. The pendulum of human likes and dislikes continues to swing sometimes in one direction and sometimes in another. Such a criterion to evaluate our actions is not a dependable and valid instrument to label the outcome of human activities good or bad.

Human likes and dislikes are purely whimsical a passing fancy. That is why many persons who were heroes of yesterday-decorated with national honours-have turned out men of dubious integrity involved in shady deals. Yesterday light was focussed on them when they were awarded but today who honoured them with a fanfare must be secretly repenting their decision.

What makes yesterday's hero today's non-entity? The answer is not difficult to find. If we apply sound logic to assess the outcome of human actions, error can be by and large eliminated and our judgement can have universal validity. A judgement is universally valid when it is based on reason (sound logic, contrary to whims). Such a judgement has divine element because reason is the shadow of God.

In simple words reason is linked with our conscience which prevents us from going wrong. We go wrong when we forget that our conscience is our best guide in the dark lanes of life. Human conscience is like a hurricane-lamp whose light never goes out even in the midst of fierce storms if man does not deliberately play mischief with it.

The difference between a good man and & bad man is that the former resists temptations and the latter surrenders with full knowledge of dangerous consequences. When bad actions become open violations, law punishes him. But many a time man uses his mental faculty to bypass law. His actions then apparently become blameless, sometimes even win applause. But in reality he is never at peace with himself. His troubled conscience inflicts self torment from which there is no escape. Such persons are gentlemen criminals.

To escape from this perpetually tormenting situation man engages himself in isolated good acts. He believes, though foolishly, that such acts will ensure his salvation (spiritual liberation). He conveniently forgets that a plant can't be kept healthy and fragrant by watering it once in a while. When nobility is crushed and morality drained out enjoyment of delicious spiritual fruit becomes a distant dream—an illusion. Light and darkness never co-exist. You can't eat your cake and have it too. Dhammapad—a famous

Buddhist Scripture says, "whoever speaks or acts with impure mind, him sorrow follows, as the wheel follows the steps of the ox that draws the cart". Self tormenting inevitably follows when purity is disturbed.

God has not created hell for man. It is man's own creation. Men do not go to hell (a symbol of suffering) because God is angry with them. Misery is the outcome of a fallen spirit. The state does not punish the law-abiding citizens. Prisons are for law-breakers. Spiritual happiness can't be enjoyed by following wrong goals. There is an old proverb: "As you sow so shall you reap. By sowing thistles you can't enjoy sweet juicy mangoes".

If a man wants to enjoy spiritual bliss he must learn to set his priorities right. Nothing is good or bad but our thinking makes it so. Hence there is need to keep our thinking—the workshop of ideas in proper order. Man is made by his belief, says the Gita. God has given man the marvellous power of thinking. Thinking means power of discrimination—the capacity to know the difference between good and bad. Thinking is the source of enlightenment. It sets man apart from animals. Thinking persuaded Balmiki to abandon the path of sin and become a saint. Thinking inspired Lord Buddha to abandon royal glory and choose the austerity which leads to spiritual happiness. God has conferred on man the greatest power—the power to choose one's own actions. You can't choose your parents. But you can choose what you wish to do. You can choose the food you wish to enjoy. You can choose the clothes you wish to wear. You can choose friends. You can choose your life-mate.

Obviously the choice of one's actions determines the quality of one's ultimate achievements. One who chooses to be an artist, a scientist, a man of letters voluntarily chooses life of austerity and hard work, quite often unrewarded hard work. His spirit of self-denial enables him to preserve the excellence of his work and his name shines in perpetual glory. He strives to enrich cultural heritage which is non-attached possession—an asset for the entire mankind. Clearly such a person is unselfish and not acquisitive.

The moment one turns acquisitive he is on the way to spiritual doom. He occasionally feels the temporary pinch for his wrong acts and then joins the crowd justifying his bad actions saying that others too are doing the same. He does not pause to think that by doing so he is murdering the divine within and thus becoming his own enemy. He does not realize that a bad person is like a raw fruit which is bitter and sour.

An acquisitive person tormented by pricks of conscience occasionally adopts gimmicks to soothe himself. He performs isolated acts of charity and piety. By doing so he poses to be idealistic—God-fearing. He feeds his ego saying "I am great because I am admired by others". But this is indeed a dangerous illusion. The society knows the drunkard and the smuggler because he goes about his work unashamedly and cares two hoots for public opinion. But a spiritual hypocrite is a different creature. He carries on his evil activities under the cloak of idealism. A spiritual hypocrite may be teetotaller, a regular visitor to a shrine but by adulterating food-stuff and by selling spurious drugs he may be killing many innocent persons.

Dharm Sutra says, "When a man practises charity in order to be reborn in heaven or for fame or reward or from fear, such charity can obtain no pure effect".

Truly speaking isolated acts of charity are an exercise in futility. Such acts are as good as a few drops of rain in the vast desert.

Worldly desires blunt man's power of discrimination and blur his spiritual vision. As a result he begins to mistake means as ends. By mere reading of scriptures he expects to become a saint, but this is not true. Practice of virtue in day to day life holds the key to spiritual bliss.

To be absorbed all the time in the world around and never turn a thought within is spiritual blindness. The first step for soul is to put away outward things and look within. Until we put an end to our attachment to material gains there can be no love for God. The soul that is attached to anything can't attain salvation. Whether it be a strong rope or a delicate thread that holds the bird, matters little until the cord is broken, the bird can't fly. So the soul held by bonds of attachment however slight they may be, can't find its way to God.

What is detachment? The state of detachment is when the heart weeps for what it has lost, the spirit laughs for what it has found. Spiritual love differs from possession of gold. Matter on distribution diminishes and finally disappears. But ideas both spiritual and intellectual get strengthened on distribution. Lord Krishna in the Gita asks Arjun to do his divinely ordaned duty without fruits of action. Kabir also says, "The devout seeker is he who mingle in his heart the double currents of love and detachment". By losing ego-centric life one gains spiritual bliss. One may say that this state is not easy to achieve. But you have to pay the price of everything. The following popular adage embodies great wisdom! "There is no sweetness without sweat".

True food for nourishment of divine life is provided by prayer and contemplation. The purpose of prayer is to teach humility and the purpose of contemplation is to focus attention on virtues like temperance and chastity. An action divorced from prayer is unenlightened and thus harmful. Action enables you to accomplish certain things. But mere accomplishment is not enough. It is the quality of accomplishment that counts.

God is by no means the only object of contemplation. On the negative side it may be money, sex and power. If One's thinking is constantly focussed on money he may become a smuggler, blackmarketeer or may indulge in other forms of corruption. One who is obsessed with sex may turn a womaniser. One who has a lust for power may turn a ruthless dictator. On the positive side comes art, literature and science. Negative contemplation is the most dangerous for society. Positive contemplation on the other hand bestows countless benefits on society.

But mere knowledge of ways to spiritual bliss is not enough. A chemist knows the names of many medicines but is ignorant of their proper application. Moreover medicine is not health. It is only a means to regain the lost health. One encounters difficulties in the pursuit of spiritual bliss when he proceeds from theory to practice.

God does not reserve salvation only for a few souls. On the contrary He finds few who permit him to work such sublime things for them. There are many who when He sends them trials shrink from the labour.

Some misuse prayer and contemplation to achieve wrong ends. The Gita says, "Most men worship the gods because they want success in their worldly undertakings". These men of small understanding pray only for what is transient and perishable.

Education plays a vital role in developing spiritual vision of man. But what is education doing to modern man? Instead of whetting his spiritual appetite it is plunging him into the whirlpool of materialism. Modern man wants more gold than God. In other words education has made him more cunning than creative. This is by no mans glorification of poverty. Man certainly can't live without bread. Poverty dehumanizes the individual and induces him to do heinous crimes. But mad pursuit of materialistic grandeur too tempts man no less to commit crimes of which he feels ashamed in moments of self-realization. Of course such moments are rare—a mere flash of lighting on a dark rainy night.

Education must transform man's acquisitiveness into non-attachment if he is keen to leave his foot-prints on sands of time. Time as everyone knows is a ruthless destroyer. But Time exempts those who display holy indifference to material goods and cultivate creativity. Their names perpetually shine in the arena of arts, literature, science and religion. Time is powerless to destroy their immortality. Indeed Time pays homage to their sacred memory.

Man stands alone in virtue and sin. A man of discrimination knowing this truth well chooses to be in the company of the virtuous and scrupulously avoids the path of sin.

Cancer of Corruption

There are numerous ways is which the monster of corruption manages to sneak into the mind of man and induces him to depart from the path of nobility.

Recently the following stirring news items appeared in national dailies:

1. Prosecution of Laloo
2. Biggest Bull Parekh held on Black Friday
3. Cricket Mired in Graft
4. Corruption in Agra University
5. Ex-chief of Customs in CBI Custody for Graft

All these screaming news items bear testimony to the fact that neither individuals nor governments nor universities which are supposed to nurture high moral values in the youth are invulnerable to the evil of corruption. Corruption which by eclipsing the sublimity in man threatens to spell disaster for society has been defined in many ways.

The Report of the Committee on Prevention of Corruption (1964) says, "In its widest connotation corruption includes improper or selfish exercise of power and influence attached to a public office or to a special position one occupies in public life." Robert C. Brooks observes, "Political corruption is a wilful failure to perform a specified duty in order to receive some direct personal gain." Elliott and

Merill remark, "Graft is the abuse of control over the power and resources of the State for the purpose of personal or party profit."

What is the modus operandi of corruption? Indeed there are numerous ways in which the monster of corruption manages to sneak into the mind of man and induces him to depart from the path of nobility. Some notable sources of corruption are discussed below:—

Nexus between big business and politics is one of the greatest sources of corruption. True, democracy is the best form of government in modern times. But huge sums of money are needed to fight an election which hardly any candidate can afford. Naturally a person with political ambitions and little money turns to a businessman to finance his election battle. Success of a candidate at the polls becomes a handy tool for the businessman to amass a vast fortune by cashing in on his influence. This is as much applicable to an individual candidates as to a political party which receives donations in several forms. If a politician who owes his electoral success to a businesshouse, says that he will not dole out patronage to it after assuming a key position in the government, he is plainly indulging in myth-making. One who pays the piper is entitled to call a tune of his own choice is an incontestable fact.

The Committee on Corruption (1964) observes "Corruption can exist only if there is someone willing to corrupt and capable of corrupting. We regret to say that both this willingness and capacity to corrupt is found in a large measure in the industrial and commercial classes."

No doubt there are some politicians who win elections without the support of big business-houses. But their number is negligible. Hence there is urgent need to take stringent measures to curb election expenses. Without taking effective measures to delink big business and politics the hope of rooting out corruption is just wishful thinking.

Increasing functions in the State are also responsible for the spread of corruption. For instance, decades ago the functions of the police were limited. But now they have multifarious duties to discharge which bring them into close contact with the public. This has unleashed the monster of corruption in the police department. In this force most people succumb to the temptation of getting easy money through bribes. Cases of corrupt police officials are often highlighted by press reports and strictures passed on them by the judiciary.

Lack of integrity among police officials is a matter of deep concern as they are entrusted with the crucial task a safe-guarding the life and property of the public. Why does a policeman go wrong? Edward D. Sullivan believes that crime is the result of collusion between a politician and a policeman. His following comment is evealing, "Actually organised crime could not exist if it were not fostered by corrupt politicians and corrupt police."

If the fence starts eating the crops one cane easily imagine the consequences. Preaching sermons can never make the police lovers of integrity. Pragmatic steps should be taken to inculcate in them true sense of service and integrity. There can be no better solution to this problem than the provision of adequate salary and housing facilities, particularly for the staff at lower level. Without improving their economic lot considerably all exhortations on integrity will prove as fruitless as rain drops in the desert. In case the evil persists despite adequate salaries exemplary punishment should be meted out to erring persons.

Graft is not confined to the police alone. For instance, people scornfully call the P.W.D. as the Public (Money) Waste Deptt. And it needs no evidence. One has just to open his eyes to see this. Even the sectional officer in the P.W.D. enjoys an elegant lifestyle which is the envy of may senior officers. Is the sectional officer gifted with supernatural powers that he can stretch his rupee infinitely? His affluence is by no means a mystery. He owes it all to his itching palm. Other departments like income tax and sales tax too are stinking with graft. To clean all those Augean stables drastic measures are needed. Without striking fear of deterrent punishment the erring persons can't be made to imbibe love of integrity.

Corruption also stems from change in values of life.

People in general have become indifferent to spiritualism and austerity. Craze for the enjoyment of fantastic material comforts is in evidence everywhere. When people find that these comforts can't be had by honest means they turn to dubious means. Malpractices like hoarding and adulteration produce instant results in swelling their coffers. No doubt while doing this they have to suppress the voice of their conscience. But they find its compensation in the enhanced social status which they come to enjoy as a result of their tremendous riches. In our society today values of life have become topsy-turvy. No wonder that virtue and talent have faded into insignificance in comparison with wealth. As a matter of fact talent and virtue have to pay a homage to the deity of affluence. This process must be reversed before we reach the stage of no return. To protect ourselves from the baneful effects of riches we must bear in mind that talent and virtue are always superior to wealth.

Today people throughout the world cherish the memory of Guru Nanak, Kabir, Tansen, Leonardo Da Vinci and Abraham Lincoln only because of their deeds. Good deeds, not affluence, pave the way to fame and immortality. To foster this awareness right type of education is needed. Observance of austerity is also a very effective antidote to curb the breeding of corruption. The President N. Sanjiva Reddy's decision to lead simple life as an indictment of those who while living in fabulous luxury exhort the destitute masses to observe austerity. Preaching without practice is like sin rebuking virtue. Lest more and more people in high places emulate the President's example this will surely have a salutary impact on people's mind and dissuade them from accumulating ill-gotten wealth.

Corruption is not peculiar to India. In his book "Ethics of Government" P. H. Douglas writes. "Corruption was rife in British public life till a hundred years ago and in USA till the beginning of this century." In British India corruption was widespread even among the high ranking officials of the East India Company. Robert Clive, the founder of the British rule in India and Lord Hastings—a Governor General of India—could not resist the temptation to make fast buck through questionable means. But they could not escape censure by their people for their misdeeds. Instead of according a red carpet welcome the British people heaped calumny on them. Recently President Nixon was caught in the web of scandals. American public did not condone his shady deals and pushed him from the peak of glory to the pit of gloom where he is sulking now. Even Gerald Ford who was Nixon's nominee to Presidency was made to lick the dust of defeat at the hustings. Inspired by America's example Indians in the last elections have hounded out a large number of politicians of doubtful integrity out of public life. This must teach a lesson to all politicians that dishonesty does not pay eventually. People one day are sure to discover the wolf in sheep's clothing.

True, dishonest politicians can be punished at the polls. But what about the dishonest people in other professions? How to bring them to book? To penalise erring persons Prevention of Corruption Act, 1947 was passed. But this legislation was not found sufficiently effective. To add teeth to it an amendment was made on the recommendations of the Bakshi Tek Chand Committee set up in 1949. This too could not tame the monster of corruption. Then the Administrative Vigilance Division was created in the Home Ministry in August 1955. But politicians remained beyond the purview of all these measure. Now the realisation has dawned that a politician however highly placed can be corruptible like any other person. Hence the measures like the creation of a Lok Pal and anti-defection bill are receiving serious attention of the Parliament.

All these measures are no doubt highly commendable to weed out corruption. But much more important than this is the need to change the human mind—the real breeding place for corruption. This task education alone can accomplish. Education today is considered as process of sharpening human mind with a view to utilising it for materialistic gains. Abnormal accent on materialistic values should be urgently rectified. Let education not squeeze the milk of human kindness out of us and thereby reduce us to robots. It is worth-while to bear in mind that a flower without fragrance has little significance. Similarly a human being obsessed with materialistic gains and showing scant respect to moral values is no better than an animal. Without the restraining influence of sound moral values one is likely to follow the disastrous dictum: "Get rich quick and kick everyone else into the ditch." Let education illumine the dark recesses of human mind. If enlightenment comes, can corruption be there? Who does not know that light and darkness can't co-exist?

Author: V. Rajesh
Format: Paperback
Language: English
Pages: 104

It is easy to skip a question during an exam if it is "Out of Syllabus" but what do you do if you are faced with a situation in life for which you were not given any inputs? Can you run away from the situation using the "Out of Syllabus" excuse?

Career is one area where one is expected to know and manage situations. After all a person is paid a salary to be able to handle things and deliver results. The reality is that most people get a lot of academic and conceptual inputs relating to one's career choice but very little practical inputs on how to effectively use the academic learning.

Author: Prof. Shrikant Prasoon
Format: Paperback
Language: English
Pages: 200

Group Discussions (GD) are commonly used to assess several personality aspects of candidates during various entrance tests and as a part of selection process for various jobs. This book can be a game changer for most students, since even most technically sound and brilliant students often falter at GD.

This comprehensive guide book helps you clear the fog surrounding GD and its step-by-step instructions will make you a winner in GD.

This book includes:

- Insight into: Need of GD, Do's & Don'ts in GD, Body Language & Public Speaking, Skills & Ability required in GD, and so on
- Important GD topics, How to gather Information for GD, Reading & Practice for GD

Author: Bibhu Prasad Mishra
Format: Paperback
Language: English
Pages: 233

The book 'Preparing for a Winning Interview' is divided into two sections. The first section deals with the preparations, research and understanding various facts of the interview and its procedure.

The second section contains understanding and learning specific job skills in ever-changing and challenging corporate environment; the role of an employee and the need to be prepared beforehand to fit in different organisation by meeting tough corporate tasks, and by coping with the changing works, conditions and milieu.

The book covers all the core areas of interview process, delicacies in work environment, intricacies of challenging spheres, the need of sustainbility, and presents ready and easy solutions.

Author: Prof. Shrikant Prasoon
Format: Paperback
Language: English
Pages: 248

Chanakya was both a destructive and creative thinker able to annihilate an established empire and erect and establish another larger, richer and greater on the debris, without money, material and man. So, he is the only qualified person in human history to be Guru; Acharya; Teacher; Guide and Mentor in the field of Management. With his super mind and supreme determination he succeeded in everything and everywhere; and wrote down everything without inhibitions or secrecy for the posterity in his three monumental works:

1. Teachings of Kautilya's Arthashastra & Nitishastra
2. Perfect Analogy between Ancient Managerial System & Modern Corporate Setup

Author: Vishal Goyal
Format: Paperback
Language: English
Pages: 228

Tenali Raman was a court jester, an intelligent advisor and one of the ashtadiggajas (elephants serving as pillars and taking care of all the eight sides) in the Bhuvana Vijayam (Royal Court) of the famed Emperor of Vijayanagar Empire (City of Joy) in Karnataka – Sri Krishna Deva Raya (1509-1529), the model ruler par excellence to Ashoka, Samudra Gupta and Harsha Vardhana. Tenali Raman was an embodiment of acute wit and humour and an admirable poet of knowledge, shrewdness and ingenuity. In a short span, the legacy left behind by Tenali Raman attained eternity. All these qualities of Tenali Raman have been fully explored and displayed in this collection of vibrant fables and anecdotes.

Author: S.P. Sharma
Format: Paperback
Language: English
Pages: 120

In a world marked by competition, personality is the key to success – whether it is social or business or personal or political arena. Interview for IAS or an MNC, meeting with the parents of your prospective bride, addressing a public rally, or delivering a speech in an international conference...if you have a confident and pleasing personality, you will surely make your mark! This book seeks to motivate young men and women, particularly students, to make conscious and continuous effort to build character and develop good personality.

visit our online bookstore: **www.vspublishers.com**

Author: Dr. Nivedita Ganguli
Format: Paperback
Language: English
Pages: 108

Do you feel that life sometimes pulls you down? Do you keep on searching for some light to pull you out of darkness? Do you feel so wrapped up in your own issues that you miss out the real treasure of life? Probably this book may create a full-stop to your search. The episodes present in the book would enable you to see life from a brighter perspective. The 'In a Nutshell' portion following each episode would give direction towards Life Management. Quotations present in form of 'Food for Thought' would give rich nutrition to your thought process. Our wrong perspective towards everyday issues makes life more complicated. Changing perspective would enable us to live life fully.

Author: Anchit Barnwal
Format: Paperback
Language: English
Pages: 168

Just as a winning podium can accommodate anyone on it, each one of us is capable to be a winner, irrespective of our shortcomings and differences. Winners' Podium – Everyone Fits on it, attempts to do just that: make out a winner amongst each one of us.

This book offers elaborate guidelines for a balanced, successful and happy living. It tells how one can find his talent, attract ideas and be successful, both personally and professionally. It also talks of happiness and the steps to it.

Through stories, anecdotes, quotations, examples and day to day observations, this book can inspire you to not only attain that most desirable success, but also to hold on and grow both internally and externally with it.

Author: Barun Roy
Format: Paperback
Language: English
Pages: 124

Journalism today is an upcoming and a popular career offering bright prospects.

This book captures the scintillating thrill, sensational excitement, and vivacious action that is associated with journalism. The career-seekers find it difficult to gain the basic knowledge and the nitty-gritty of this highly electric and charged life. To fill in this void and fulfil the curiosity of such readers, this book has come up as a solution and has gained immense popularity solely because it is a comprehensive and impressive book dealing with all aspects of media.

It envelops all the facets and streams related to journalism in a succinct presentation.

visit our online bookstore: **www.vspublishers.com**

Author: Suniti Chandra Mishra

Format: Paperback

Language: English

Pages: 168

It is a unique book dedicated to all those individuals who have a burning desire in their heart to write profitably. The author has discussed 11 powerful ingredients that will help one become a prolific writer. The instructions will greatly enhance the reader's writing quality and is meant to make his road to success as a writer less jerky.

The book further discusses how world-class writers have overcome their drawbacks through sheer hard work, patience, determination and will. The great writers of the past all believed in themselves and their writings poured from their heart.

The Assignments and Exercises at the end of each chapter are designed in a way that will enable the reader to test his/her understanding and applicability of what he/she has learnt.

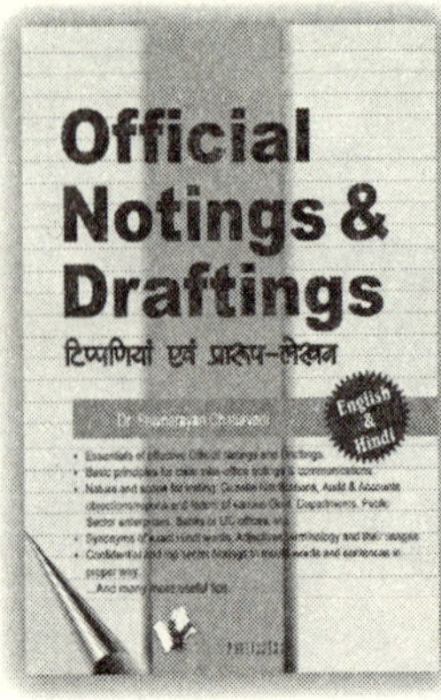

Author: Dr. Shivnarayan Chaturvedi

Format: Paperback

Language: English

Pages: 131

This authoritative book has been a sincere effort of the author who worked for 23 years in the Hindi Department of the Lal Bahadur Shastri Administrative Academy, Mussoorie. Hindi is both the National and the official language of India since independence. Hindi is the mother tongue of the majority — approximately 450 million Indians.

Ever since Hindi gained the status of the official language, the moral responsibility of making the language acceptable in all administrative forms has gradually increased. For the growth, development and expansion of Hindi, 'Official Notings and Drafting' is a positive endeavour.

Author: Gerard Assey

Format: Paperback

Language: English

Pages: 124

The book details the basics of frontline sales management and broadly covers all aspects of managerial skills – presented by a veteran with over two decades of experience in sales and sales management. The topics include range from managing oneself in terms of time and priorities, to setting goals, interviewing sales personnel, importance of training and conducting training workshops, delegation, problem-solving, managing meetings, caring for the customer and a lot more.

The book will empower sales managers with winning strategies on various aspects of management applicable to any type of organisation, regardless of the product or service.

visit our online bookstore: **www.vspublishers.com**

Author: Prem P Balla
Format: Paperback
Language: English
Pages: 175

Every man aspires to project an image of poise, positivity and personal charm. But few men really know how to achieve this. In this context, The Portrait of a Complete Man acts as an indispensable guidebook.

The book gives pointers that include: the power of perseverance and positivity; developing personal magnetism, poise and manners; cultivating healthy habits; tackling personal and sexual problems; enjoying love, marriage and fatherhood; succeeding at the workplace; handling people; improving efficiency; recognising the importance of recreation; and growing old gracefully.

The book gives practical guidelines on how a man can discover peace, happiness and contentment and become complete perfect.

Author: Aparna Chattoupadhyay
Format: Paperback
Language: English
Pages: 176

This fascinating book authored by Dr. Aparna Chattopadhyay, offers you a new vision of self-awareness which would enable you to assess your feelings, capabilites and aptitudes. As you develop self-awareness, you will not only be able to identify the emotional pattern in your life and manage then well, but will also be able to activate all-round personality development.

It will help lead life more powerfully than before through a wide range of psychological quizzes.

This book enables you to:

- Generate fresh enthusiasm and ambition in your life
- Live more happily and effectively
- Build self-confidence and develop inner peace
- Enjoy better interpersonal relationship

Author: Aparna Chattoupadhyay
Format: Paperback
Language: English
Pages: 176

A better insight into the dynamics of achieving success in one's job and business is the need of the hour. Success when viewed with a positive mental attitude, is a process. It is a journey - not the destination. Explore your own road to success by analysing, recognising, visualising and mobilising traits.

This self-help book gives you new ways of energising your hidden qualities, potentials and possibilities of success in your business and career arenas to :

- Harness creativity and enthusiasm to work more productively and successfully.
- Identify your leadership strengths.
- Develop skills of management.

Author: Surendra Dogra 'Nirdosh'

Format: Paperback

Language: English

Pages: 112

Have you ever thought of addressing an audience and making them listen to you without batting an eyelid? Do you want to create a trance-like spell on people listening to your speech?

It has carefully dissected every aspect of public speaking and presents a clear map that any aspiring speaker can follow. Besides, it also incorporates the necessary techniques to motivate, captivate, and persuade the audience while making various presentations, etc.

You will master 'How to'

- Conquer stage fright
- Organize material in a flowing manner
- Customise speech for different sets of gathering
- Inspire audience

Author: Vinay Mohan Sharma

Format: Paperback

Language: English

Pages: 120

Communication is not always through sound or language. Much can be said with gestures or movement of eyes. In fact, more often than not, the Body Language says more than words.

Now discover all the finer points and nuances of body language in this masterly work:

- How thumb gesture displays dominance, superiority and aggression
- How dilation of eyes sends romantic signal
- How a sideways glance indicates either hostility or interest

Author: Carani N. Rao

Format: Paperback

Language: English

Pages: 124

The purpose of this book is to share with the readers the 10 fundamental rules to achieve success compiled from the vast ocean of literature on success. Some of these essential rules include – setting a goal, positive attitude and self confidence, purposeful desire, planning and preparation, resources, inputs, discipline, action, persistence or perseverance, prayer and values.

Here success is first defined; then the basic rules involved in achieving success are enumerated and explained with relevant anecdotes and stories. Besides these 10 fundamental rules, a set of success formulae as well as virtue capsules have also been added in the book.

Author: Seema Gupta
Format: Paperback
Language: English
Pages: 156

The book deals exhaustively with the varied nuances of etiquette and good manners for all important occasions.

A handy guide for all age-groups to constantly cultivate the acumen of polished behaviour to outshine in all spheres of life.

Children are inquisitive and imitative by nature. Let their perception absorb the bonhomie, cheerfulness and courtesy all around for an overall growth of their personalities.

All the important aspects of tricky situations and how to handle them have been dealt with in detail. Posture, building relationships, communication skills – to mention just a few. Each instance merits discretion and tact.

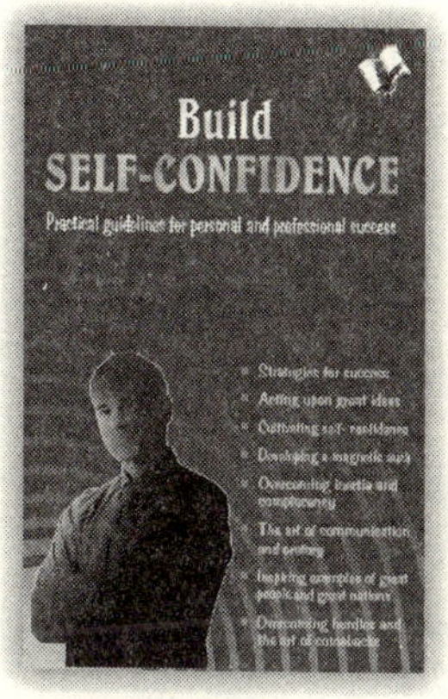

Author: Alankrita
Format: Paperback
Language: English
Pages: 120

Life is never a bed of roses. However, if we know how to negotiate our way between the thorns and hurdles of life, the roses of success will be ours for selective picking. The greatest asset in the quest for success and happiness is our measure of self-confidence. More than half of all life's battles are won or lost in the mind. Therefore, a person needs to saturate his or her mind with positive thoughts at all times.

The book is liberally sprinkled with myriad stories, anecdotes and events that inspire us to follow in the footsteps of those who achieved greatness. It teaches you how to overcome old habits and encumbrances on your journey to the highest peaks and how to mould your circumstances, rather than be moulded by them.

Author: S.P. Sharma
Format: Paperback
Language: English
Pages: 176

The author of this book, S.P. Sharma, not only discusses the problems faced by modern man in this book, but also explains certain religious truths in a comprehensive manner in non-technical language.

It contains useful information designed to help one relieve from anxiety and disturbing thoughts – providing a clear vision leading to a happier life.

It would help one:

- Combat the shocks of life
- Know that nothing is more useful than the awakened self
- Understand the principles that make life happier

It is a wonderful work for anyone who desires to get Success Through Positive Thinking.

Author: Prem P. Bhalla
Format: Paperback
Language: English
Pages: 143

Exams play a major role in the lives of not just students, but adults too. Although youngsters are taught a variety of subjects to equip them for adult life, no school teaches them how to excel in exams. Most learn through trial and error. Others remain clueless about how to excel in exams. This crucial information if learnt can ensure that even those with average IQ excel in exams.

This book contains simple and practical tips and guidelines on how to tap your full potential and give off your best during exams. An invaluable guide for everyone due to appear in exams. It is equally useful for parents who wish to ensure their children do well and secure maximum marks.

Author: Abhishek Thakore
Format: Paperback
Language: English
Pages: 142

Success today depends a lot on one's academic achievements. And to excel in studies, you don't have to be just an intelligent or brilliant student — but also one who knows how to manage studies and time. In fact, even a mediocre or a below-average student can perform exceedingly well by following a scientific system.

The Portrait of a Super Student now brings you an innovative system, specifically designed for super achievement. From simple, practical and time-tested tips on how to manage time, controlling temptation, scheduling time and work, relaxing techniques to diet control, speed reading, building vocabulary, improving presentation, discussing studies.

Author: B.K. Narayan & Preeti Narayan
Format: Paperback
Language: English
Pages: 133

251 Study Secrets from the Diary of a Top Achiever provides you easy methods and tricks to achieve success in studies—without stress and tension. This unique 'quick help' book for students explains with all the topics that are important for your study success. Here are some of the topics:

- Confidence
- Motivation
- Choosing Career
- Fixing Goal in Mind
- Increasing Brainpower
- Programme to Succeed
- Concentration

This book is written in short, concise form so that you can read fast, learn quickly, and use instantly! If you need more help visit: www.mindpowerguide.biz

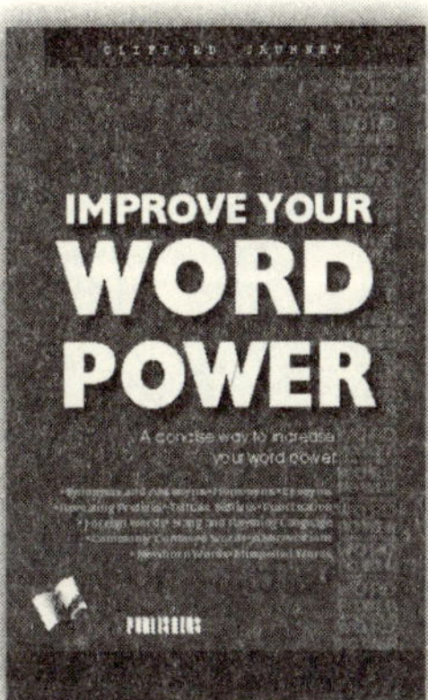

Author: Califord Sawhney
Format: Paperback
Language: English
Pages: 230

English language has benefitted from innumerable poets and authors, from the past as well as the present, who have contributed profusely to its rich heritage. Nonetheless, we can not ignore the complexities of the English language which sometimes perplex a reader or even a scholar. *Improve your Word Power* by Clifford Sawhney simplifies all these complexities by providing answers to the many nagging grammatical queries, syntax, style, choice of words, spellings, etc. This book serves as a complete guide that elaborately explains the usages of nouns, adjectives, adverbs, phrases, proverbs and so on. Hence, it will undoubtedly serve as a bible for both the lovers and wizards of English language.

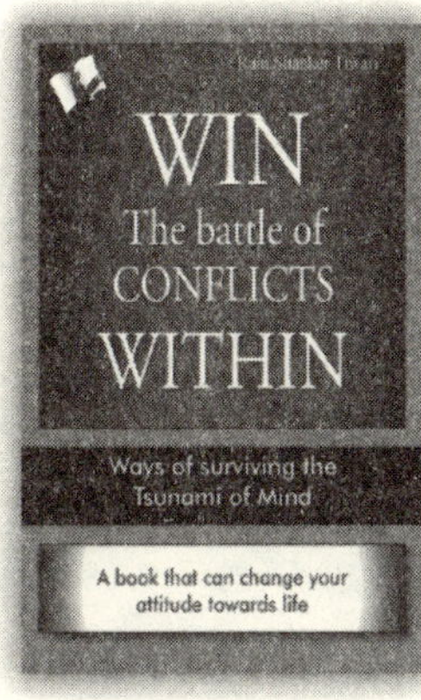

Author: Ram Shanker Tiwari
Format: Paperback
Language: English
Pages: 260

Our intellect creates our Karma. Our wild desires and ego produce conflicts by absurd and self-contradictory demands. Hence we remain unhappy and agitated even though we may possess enormous prosperity and power! Such a 'Battle of conflicts within' goes on all through life and we are tossed in the tsunami "tornado of our longings in the mind". How to attain tranquil, happiness, stable fulfilment and the purpose of our coming to this planet, the earth? Herein the wisdom of the Ancient, an analysis of the Self, connected with the source of power and total alteration of our attitude towards our life have been blended together to achieve practical as well as spiritual enlightenment.

Author: Dr B.R. Suhas
Format: Paperback
Language: English
Pages: 187

Immortal Sayings is a collection of Subhashitas. These sayings reveal a simple, down-to-earth philosophy and convey important morals and messages for the common people with enlightening examples drawn from Nature. Kalidasa, Bhavabhuti, Kalhana, Bhartrihari and other celebrated ancient poets and writers.

The Subhashitas have been compiled from the Vedas, Upanishads, Mahabharata, Ramayana, Puranas, Panchatantra, Hitopadesha, Neeti Shashtra and other celebrated works. Besides being enjoyable reading, Immortal Sayings shows the path to true happiness and contentment.